"The margin between AI hype and substance is extremely thin. But *AI Innovation in Business* cuts right through the AI hype and offers a clear, practitioner-ready playbook. Timely, grounded, insightful, and immediately useful—Jonny Holmström wrote the concise guide managers need to create sustainable value from AI."

Jan Recker, *Professor, University of Hamburg*

"A sharp and inspiring take on the AI-first paradigm, Holmström's book positions AI as a 'generative engine' reshaping how organizations think and act. Through the organizational, relational, and ecosystem views, it captures the profound shift toward an AI-first world where intelligence drives every layer of value creation, where machine learning is at the core of business strategy."

Carl Piva, *CEO, The Swedish Internet Foundation*

"As an accomplished digital innovation researchers and close collaborator with industry leaders, Holmström has over the past decade developed cutting-edge knowledge about the opportunities and challenges afforded by AI. His recent book *AI Innovation in Business* presents the key insights from these efforts, in an easy to read and comprehensive form that professionals, entrepreneurs and executives will find engaging, provocative and useful. It is a must read."

Lars Mathiassen, *Professor, Georgia State University*

AI Innovation in Business

Unlike many AI books that take a purely technical or cheerleading angle, this book bridges strategy, management, technology, and policy to demystify the AI revolution and tackle the urgent question facing today's leaders: How can we truly unlock value from AI?

Championing an ecosystem approach, Jonny Holmström reveals that capturing AI's full value is not just a technical hurdle but a strategic and organizational challenge that demands new ways of thinking and collaborating beyond the walls of any single company. Readers will discover how an ecosystem approach – coordinating efforts across departments, companies, and even industries – can turn isolated AI experiments into transformative business value. Blending real-world case studies, cutting-edge research, and pragmatic frameworks, the book provides a roadmap to sustainable AI innovation, from preparing your organization for AI ("AI readiness") to forging data strategies and addressing ethical dilemmas.

For business leaders, IT professionals, and policymakers alike, this is essential reading for those looking to harness AI's potential responsibly and strategically – not merely as a tool, but as a catalyst for reinventing the future of business.

Jonny Holmström is a renowned scholar and advisor at the forefront of digital innovation and AI management. He serves as a Professor of Informatics at Umeå University in Sweden, where he co-founded and directs the Swedish Center for Digital Innovation (SCDI), a leading interdisciplinary research center that collaborates with industry to advance digital transformation knowledge. Over a career spanning two decades, Dr. Holmström has built an international reputation for bridging academic insights with real-world impact.

AI Innovation in Business

How Artificial Intelligence Can Create Value for Organizations

Jonny Holmström

Routledge
Taylor & Francis Group
NEW YORK AND LONDON

Designed cover image: Credit: Jonny Holmström

First published 2026
by Routledge
605 Third Avenue, New York, NY 10158

and by Routledge
4 Park Square, Milton Park, Abingdon, Oxon, OX14 4RN

Routledge is an imprint of the Taylor & Francis Group, an informa business

ISBN: 978-1-041-22776-2 (hbk)
ISBN: 978-1-041-22775-5 (pbk)
ISBN: 978-1-003-73388-1 (ebk)

DOI: 10.4324/9781003733881

Typeset in Times New Roman
by Deanta Global Publishing Services, Chennai, India

Access the Support Material: www.routledge.com/9781041227755

Contents

Preface

The rules of business have changed. In every industry, the spread of new AI technologies and the rise of new opportunities and threats associated with new AI are transforming organizations across the globe. The AI revolution has turned the old business playbook upside down. In my own work, teaching and advising business leaders from organizations around the world, I repeatedly hear the same urgent question: How can organizations create value from AI?

In pursuing the answer to this question, I have been privileged to draw on the insights, perspectives, and questions of an amazing range of executives and entrepreneurs, both through my consulting and in my role as a researcher. I have also been privileged to draw on the insights from my students when we have jointly explored the opportunities and challenges associated with new forms of AI. In these discussions, one central insight emerged and shaped the development of this entire book: AI transformation is not only about technology – it is also about strategy and new ways of thinking. Transforming for the age of AI requires your business to upgrade its strategic mindset much more than its AI infrastructure. This is apparent in the changing roles of technology leadership within business. A Chief Information Officer's traditional role has been to use technology to optimize processes, reduce risks, and better run the existing business. But the emerging role of a Chief Digital Officer in the age of AI is much more strategic, focused on using technology to reimagine and reinvent the core business itself.

To succeed in the age of AI is a huge challenge, as the rise of AI already has led to a number of significant transformations in various industries. In an era where AI technologies are likely to disrupt everything from education to healthcare, organizations will need new tools and capabilities. In terms of technology, AI has enabled the development of advanced machine learning algorithms and natural language processing (NLP) techniques, leading to the creation of more intelligent and autonomous systems. This has resulted in a wide range of applications, including AI assistants and automated decision-making systems. In terms of employment, the increased use of AI has led to the automation of many tasks that were previously performed by humans, leading to concerns about job displacement and the need for retraining and upskilling. Additionally, there are well-grounded concerns about the ethical and societal implications of AI, such as issues related to privacy and bias. In terms of business, AI has led to increased efficiency and automation, enabling organizations to analyze large amounts of data and make better decisions. It also allows for personalized customer experiences and new business models. Pursuing these discussions is essential to navigating the complexities and challenges posed by AI. This is a key focus of my book, where I will explore these issues in detail, elaborating on strategies to harness AI's benefits while addressing its potential drawbacks.

The pervasive nature of digital technologies in general, and AI in particular, has transformed the ways in which we organize and innovate. AI is characterized by generativity, meaning it is inherently dynamic, malleable, and context agnostic. Generative AI, like OpenAI's GPT model, can lead to value creation for organizations if managed properly, as it can drive innovation, productivity, and efficiency across multiple aspects of their operations. However, the open-endedness of digital technologies creates a two-fold challenge for organizations in managing value processes and outcomes. First, the architecture of AI technologies allows for a near-limitless recombination of data, making AI management overwhelmingly complex. To address this challenge, organizations need to adopt a proactive approach in exploring and experimenting with various AI applications, continuously refining them to align with the organization's strategy and often also the customer needs. Second, as value creation increasingly occurs at the intersection of multiple domains, effective collaboration between stakeholders becomes crucial in navigating these challenges and fostering a well-working environment for generative AI-driven innovation and transformation.

Previous research has provided only partial answers on how organizations navigate these challenges, often focusing on generativity as an enabler, and how new possibilities emerge. In recent years, a new breed of value creation enabled by AI technologies has emerged. This new breed is largely characterized by the generativity of AI technology, which has resulted in the pervasive penetration of digital technology uses in all spheres of organizations' operations, including products, services, and customer experience. Generativity, in this context, can broadly be understood as a system's capacity to create or produce new and innovative outcomes beyond its original design.

In response to increasing calls to better understand these new circumstances, it is crucial for organizations to manage AI effectively. By addressing these challenges, organizations can harness the full potential of generative AI, unlocking value creation and achieving sustainable growth in an increasingly competitive AI landscape. In the context of this book, value creation through AI is posited as a paradigm-shifting potential that AI holds for organizations. It is the idea that when AI is strategically managed, it can catalyze a level of value generation far beyond marginal enhancements or traditional growth expectations. This potential is described as paradigm-shifting due to its capacity to continually drive innovation and efficiency, crossing previously insurmountable barriers and unlocking exponential benefits. Value creation from AI frames how AI contributes to organizational growth in ways that are not just incremental but transformative. When AI is leveraged effectively, it can lead to substantial leaps in innovation, efficiency, and overall value generation. This notion is considered paradigm-shifting because the potential for AI to enhance an organization's operations and offerings is not seen as having a clear upper limit. Unlike conventional tools and methods, which may offer predictable or linear improvements, AI can break through previous limitations, enabling a company to realize growth and capabilities that may have once seemed unachievable. In practical terms, value creation from AI might involve the development of new products, services, or business models that were not possible before AI's integration. It can also manifest as AI-driven insights that lead to significant cost reductions, productivity boosts, or market advantages. Overall, it emphasizes an innovative mindset where AI is not just a support tool but a transformative agent that can redefine what an organization is capable of achieving.

AI's potential for value creation hinges on three core attributes of AI:

Adaptability: AI systems are distinguished by their ability to learn from data, adjust to new circumstances without explicit reprogramming, and evolve their performance over time. This adaptability means that AI applications can stay relevant and effective even as contextual dimensions change.

Scalability: AI technologies are inherently scalable, capable of expanding their scope and capacity with minimal additional costs. This scalability enables organizations to amplify the impact of AI across various operational areas and geographic markets without proportional increases in costs.

Collaborative Networks: AI's ability to facilitate and enhance collaboration creates network effects that amplify value. By connecting people, systems, and organizations, AI can create synergies, driving collective innovation that extends beyond the confines of individual organizations.

By leveraging these qualities, AI can serve as a key driver for an organization's transformation and competitive advantage. It can open up new opportunities for business models, create previously unimagined products and services, and foster partnerships that lead to shared success. Value creation through AI, therefore, is not just about the direct application of AI technologies but also about the broader, systemic changes they can trigger beyond organizational boundaries.

Organizations across the globe are engaged in efforts toward value creation through AI and, in some cases, we can see how organizations operate by enhancing value creation through automation, augmentation, and data exploration.

Automation through AI: AI technologies are significantly impacting organizational operations by automating processes. This automation contributes to organizational goals by improving efficiency, reducing costs, and enabling faster decision-making.

Augmentation with AI: Beyond automation, AI is also used to augment human capabilities. This involves the effective integration of human and AI systems, enhancing human work rather than replacing it. This synergy between human and machine intelligence leads to improved performance, creativity, and decision-making.

Exploring Data as a Resource: AI technologies play a crucial role in helping organizations explore and utilize data as a valuable resource. By analyzing large volumes of data, AI provides insights that were previously inaccessible, aiding in strategic decision-making and revealing new opportunities for growth and innovation.

From a managerial perspective, AI technologies are not just tools but resources that can be orchestrated for value creation. This involves identifying, developing, and leveraging these resources to achieve competitive advantages and organizational goals. Managers play a critical role in deploying AI technologies, while data scientists emerge as key figures in bridging the gap between technical potential and strategic implementation. Data scientists are instrumental in setting up AI models and guiding managerial activities in AI projects, thus driving value creation through AI in organizations. Throughout this book, I argue that a shift in management thinking is needed: capturing AI's full value calls for joint orchestration of innovation across an ecosystem, not just within a single enterprise. However, clear guidance on how to manage AI-powered innovation in an ecosystem setting remains limited. This lack of frameworks and models means that practitioners are often unsure how to build the partnerships, governance structures, and shared resources necessary for AI ecosystems to thrive. As a result, many AI initiatives underperform or remain trapped in pilot stages, never realizing the transformative impact that a coordinated ecosystem approach can achieve.

This concept is not just about financial gain for the organizations driving AI initiatives, but covers a wide spectrum of potential benefits associated with AI use in an organization, including enhanced customer experiences, innovative product development, and improved decision-making processes – made possible by automation, augmentation, and data exploration. In addition to efforts targeting the realization of such benefits, addressing challenges such as data privacy, model bias, and the digital skills gap is also crucial for organizations to realize value creation. By managing these challenges proactively and fostering a culture of continuous learning, innovation, and ethical AI use, organizations can harness value creation from AI.

In the context of this book, a driving motivation is that AI is becoming increasingly integrated into various aspects of society, and it is likely to continue to have a significant impact on how we live and work in the future. However, it is critical that we properly understand the opportunities and challenges associated with AI in order to create well-working socio-technical arrangements building on human and machine capabilities. A key issue in this effort is to understand the key challenges associated with the rise of AI for organizations and society as a whole, which includes:

Job displacement: As AI systems become more advanced, they may be able to perform tasks that were previously done by humans, leading to job loss and economic disruption.
Bias and fairness: AI systems can perpetuate and even amplify existing biases in society, leading to unfair outcomes for certain groups.
Explainability: AI systems can be opaque, making it difficult for people to understand how they make decisions, which can make it hard to trust the decisions they make.
Regulation: With the increase of AI usage, governments are struggling to create laws and regulations that can effectively govern the use of AI in a way that balances the benefits and risks.

These are indeed huge challenges, but also opportunities for organizations succeeding in dealing with these issues. In meeting with organizations trying to figure out how to work with AI, I have found that it is critical for them to be aware of these issues and also to figure out how to proactively address them to be able to create value from AI.

Doing so is far from trivial. Indeed, when organizations confront the multifaceted challenges presented by AI, such as job displacement and bias, they simultaneously engage with opportunities for transformative growth. Job displacement, a significant concern as AI systems assume roles previously held by humans, compels organizations to redefine the workforce landscape. In addressing this challenge, they ideally unlock the opportunity to foster a culture of continuous learning and innovation, guiding their employees toward more complex and creatively fulfilling roles, which can enhance job satisfaction and drive economic growth. Another bleaker scenario is, of course, that job opportunities will disappear, not to be replaced with new types of job opportunities. Similarly, the issue of bias and fairness in AI systems provides an impetus for organizations to pioneer fair and equitable AI practices. The opacity of AI decision-making processes presents a significant hurdle in gaining the trust of stakeholders, yet it also serves as a catalyst for investment in explainable AI. This pursuit not only aligns with emerging demands for transparency but also satisfies a growing market for user-friendly AI solutions that help to demystify complex algorithms, thereby building user trust and widening user engagement. As for the evolving landscape of AI regulation, while challenging in its complexity, it offers forward-thinking organizations a chance to influence policy development. By contributing to the regulatory conversation, organizations can ensure that new frameworks enable rather than stifle innovation, thus establishing themselves as responsible leaders in the field.

In essence, the interconnected nature of these challenges and opportunities prompts organizations to engage in a delicate balance of mitigating risks and embracing innovative practices. Success in this endeavor means not only surviving in an AI future but also shaping it. A key argument in this book is that the rise of AI in today's society must be accompanied by a rise in AI management skills, to create value from AI in organizations and society in a mindful way. Against this backdrop, *AI Innovation in Business: How Artificial Intelligence Can Create Value for Organizations* is a comprehensive examination of the impact of AI on the way organizations operate and compete. The book argues that the adoption of AI is having a significant impact on the way organizations make decisions and manage their operations. As AI technologies become more advanced and more widely adopted, they will limit the choices available to organizations in terms of their strategy and management practices.

The book is divided into seven parts:

1. ***From AI to Digital Transformation:*** This section explores how AI is driving digital transformation in businesses and changing the way organizations compete.
2. ***AI and data work:*** This section examines how data work is needed in order for organizations to make better and faster decisions when using AI, and how it is affecting the ways in which organizations are managed.
3. ***AI in an organizational context: Rethinking the organization:*** This section looks at how AI is impacting the traditional organization and its management structure, and the implications this has for the future of work.
4. ***AI readiness:*** This section looks at AI readiness – what it is, how it is impacting traditional organizations, and how it can be improved.
5. ***Data strategy and AI strategy:*** This section explores how data is key for any and all AI initiatives, and how data strategy and AI strategy may be approached.
6. ***AI in society:*** This section explores the broader societal implications of the rise of AI, including its effects on employment, inequality, and ethical considerations.
7. ***Creating value from AI**:* This section summarizes the key findings and conclusions from the previous sections and presents a management agenda for navigating the opportunities and challenges of AI in the organizational context. The chapter provides practical recommendations for managers and organizations on how to effectively leverage AI to drive innovation and growth, while also addressing potential risks and ensuring responsible AI practices. It also highlights future trends and areas of research in the field of AI and its impact on management, providing a roadmap for leaders to stay ahead in the age of AI.

Continuing a theme from my own research program for many years, in this book, I will return to a central question: How can organizations truly create value from AI? Of all the topics I discuss from day to day, this one is the most emotionally charged for today's managers. Over and over again, I see managers who desperately want to create value from AI. And yet they are continually frustrated by the ways in which they are coming up short in this effort. The pursuit of value creation through AI is not only a technical challenge but also a strategic endeavor that carries with it emotional significance for today's managers. They are eager to harness the capabilities of AI, yet often encounter barriers that prevent them from realizing its full potential. This book aims to explore the central question of how organizations can truly extract value from AI – a topic that is charged with urgency in the modern business environment.

Managers find themselves in a paradoxical situation where the promise of AI is palpable, yet the practicalities of implementing AI in a way that creates value are daunting. The friction stems from a multitude of factors – from misaligned strategies and insufficient infrastructure to a lack of understanding of AI's capabilities and its integration into existing organizational processes.

The book challenges the traditional, step-by-step incremental approach to business growth, instead proposing a radical paradigm where AI serves as a key driver of change. When AI is incorporated thoughtfully and in alignment with an organization's goals, it can initiate a higher level of value. The impact of AI is not confined to mere financial gains. It extends to vastly improving customer experiences, accelerating the pace and quality of innovation, and establishing a sustainable competitive edge that can endure market fluctuations. By embracing AI, then, organizations can fundamentally restructure their value chains, introducing efficiencies and capabilities that disrupt existing market dynamics and open opportunities for entirely new business models. The book recognizes the complexities and challenges that managers encounter when attempting to integrate AI into their strategic plans and daily operations. It provides them with a set of practical, actionable strategies to weave AI into the very fabric of their organizations. This integration involves a systemic approach that not only incorporates the technological aspects but also considers the human element, optimizes processes, and nurtures a culture conducive to innovation. Furthermore, for policymakers, the book sheds light on the far-reaching effects of AI beyond the organizational level. It underscores the need for ecosystems that foster AI development and adoption, which include educational initiatives, cutting-edge research, supportive regulatory environments, and robust infrastructures.

This book acts as a roadmap for both business leaders and policymakers. It provides essential knowledge and tools to effectively harness AI's potential. The call to action is clear: to recognize and seize AI's potential not merely as a technological tool but as an element that will shape the future landscape of business, opening up for value creation.

Chapter 1

From AI to digital transformation

How to avoid the AI experimentation trap

AI adoption looks very different across organizations, and a big part of that has to do with whether they have the right skills and can actually fit AI into how they already work. One of the toughest hurdles is turning AI from something that works in a pilot or test environment into something that is useful in real-world, day-to-day operations. While many organizations are eager to explore what AI can do – especially for things like smarter decision-making and automating complex tasks – they often get stuck in what I call the "experimentation trap." This happens when companies focus heavily on pilots and proof-of-concept projects but do not have a plan for scaling them up or making them part of the broader organization.

This trap creates several problems. First, experimental AI projects often do not get the resources or attention they need from leadership to move forward. That can lead to a disconnect between what these projects do and what the organization actually wants to achieve. Second, these projects are often siloed – they do not connect well with the company's existing systems, processes, or teams. That lack of integration makes it hard to see real improvements or innovations. Third, when AI stays in the pilot phase, employees do not get the chance to build the skills they need to use it effectively or work alongside it, which only deepens the skills gap over time. Lastly, experimenting without scaling can waste both money and momentum – AI requires real investment in tools, data, and people, and if those investments don't turn into real results, it is hard to justify them as anything more than expensive experiments.

To move past this, organizations need to be more strategic in the ways in which they use AI as a resource. That means tying AI efforts to actual business goals, making sure new tools can be folded into existing workflows, and investing in helping people build the skills they'll need to work with AI. It also means having a clear plan for how successful experiments will be scaled and sustained. Only then can companies avoid the experimentation trap and turn AI into something that really delivers value in a wider sense. For the purpose of this book, I look for the wider context in the so-called AI ecosystem. I define an AI ecosystem as the interconnected network of people, technologies, and institutions

DOI: 10.4324/9781003733881-1

that make AI solutions possible. This includes the organizations building and using AI, but also the infrastructure, education, and policies that support them. Thinking about AI in ecosystem terms is important because no single company can do it all alone – real value comes from working together, sharing resources, and building systems that reinforce one another. Innovation happens faster and at a greater scale when it is supported by a broader environment that is ready for it.

With that in mind, managing AI is not just a tech issue – it is a strategic one. In the rest of this section, we will dig into how AI creates value and the conditions that help or hinder that process. We will look at what AI can and can't do, what it means for jobs and skills, and how it is reshaping the way work gets done. The goal is to give you a grounded, realistic picture of AI's role in today's digital transformation – and what that means for organizations and society more broadly.

What AI can and cannot do

AI began gaining traction in organizations during the 1980s and 1990s through expert and rule-based systems that supported decision-making in areas like finance, manufacturing, and logistics. The 2000s saw a major shift with the rise of machine learning and big data, enabling AI to analyze large datasets and learn from patterns. This led to a wave of powerful applications, including natural language processing, image recognition, recommendation systems, and autonomous vehicles.

Today's organizations often struggle to digitize processes essential for AI adoption. A lack of specialized skills – especially in traditionally low-tech sectors – further hinders progress. Aligning AI with strategic goals requires not only technical adaptation but also deep organizational understanding, often involving complex digital transformation and process redesign. Cultural resistance to AI-driven decision-making, compounded by weak leadership or unsupportive environments, can stall AI initiatives. Thus, while AI holds transformative promise, its success depends on more than isolated experiments. It requires robust digital infrastructure, targeted skill development, a strategic outlook, and a culture that supports innovation. Without these, AI's potential remains largely unrealized. When dealing with the role of AI in the organizational context, we should remind ourselves that AI's role in organizations and society has been a topic of interest and discussion for many years, which is important to recall when considering the recent surge in hype. Its presence and influence can be traced back to the mid-20th century, when the concept of AI was first introduced. Over the years, AI has evolved and expanded, both in terms of its theoretical underpinnings and practical applications (for a discussion, see Russell & Norvig, 2002).

Since the inception of AI, researchers and practitioners have been exploring its potential to transform various aspects of society. Early AI research focused on developing algorithms and systems that could mimic human intelligence and problem-solving capabilities. This research laid the groundwork for AI's gradual integration into various sectors. During the 1980s and 1990s, AI began to make its presence felt in organizations, as expert systems and rule-based systems were developed to support decision-making processes. These systems were used in fields such as finance, manufacturing, and logistics, providing organizations with new tools to improve their efficiency and effectiveness. The emergence of machine learning and big data in the 2000s marked a significant shift in the AI landscape. With the ability to analyze massive datasets and "learn" from the patterns and relationships within them, AI systems became more powerful and versatile. This increased capability led to a new wave of AI applications, from natural language processing and image recognition to recommendation systems and autonomous vehicles.

Despite the recent hype surrounding AI, it is important to recognize that its role in organizations and society has been a long-standing and evolving topic. As AI continues to develop, it is likely to become even more ingrained in our lives, influencing the way we work and interact with the world around us. The challenge for organizations, governments, and individuals will be to harness AI's potential benefits while mitigating its potential risks and unintended consequences. In his seminal book "What Computers Can't Do," Hubert Dreyfus (1972) argued that AI is limited in its ability to understand context and perform tasks that require common sense. Specifically, he claimed that AI is not capable of tasks that involve human-like perception, feeling, or understanding, such as recognizing sarcasm or irony, or understanding the implications of a conversation. Dreyfus also argued that AI is not capable of making ethical or moral decisions, as it lacks the ability to understand the human experience. Since Dreyfus's seminal work, the limitations of AI have been widely scrutinized (e.g. Amoore, 2020; Crawford, 2021). Nevertheless, considering AI's rapid rise in all facets of society, it deserves more detailed critical scrutiny to make sense of the associated opportunities as well as challenges.

AI has traditionally struggled with tasks requiring human-like perception, emotion, or contextual understanding, but it excels at pattern recognition and data processing. It has long been effective in areas like image and speech recognition, language translation, and games like chess. AI also supports data-driven decision-making, such as fraud detection and stock market forecasting. Notably, Dreyfus once claimed that AI would never beat a chess grandmaster – a view disproven when Deep Blue defeated Garry Kasparov in 1997. Since then, AI capabilities have advanced significantly.

Since Deep Blue's victory over Kasparov, AI development has not merely progressed; it has accelerated at a pace that often outstrips human forecasting. Today's AI systems are not only dominating games with well-defined rules (such as chess) but are also making significant inroads into areas requiring nuanced understanding and creativity, such as language translation, content creation, and even driving vehicles. This continuous and rapid evolution of AI compels a reassessment of our preconceptions about the limitations of AI. Our thinking about AI needs to evolve in tandem with AI's capabilities, not only to understand its potential but also to identify the challenges and opportunities that come with it. We must broaden our perspectives on what AI can do and its impact on society, the economy, and the nature of work. As such, AI's growth calls for an adaptive, forward-thinking approach that anticipates changes, fosters innovation, and prepares for the practical implications of a future where AI is ubiquitous. It is not enough to be reactive; we must be visionary in our strategies and frameworks to harness the power of AI while safeguarding human values and societal well-being.

Recently, with the advancements in generative AI, such as OpenAI's GPT model, we are seeing a rise of AI that can generate human-like text and images, and it is showing an increasing ability to understand and work with context. This means that while certain limitations of AI still exist, the increasing capabilities of generative AI are expanding the scope of what is possible for AI to achieve. Generative AI refers to a type of AI that can generate new and original content, such as text, images, and even code. As noted before, one of the most well-known examples of generative AI is OpenAI's GPT model, a model that can generate human-like text. The GPT model has been trained on a huge dataset of text and can generate text that is difficult to distinguish from text written by a human. This has led to many applications in areas such as chatbots, content creation, and even coding.

The sophisticated capabilities associated with the GPT model have sparked a global conversation, stirring both excitement and controversy. Its human-like text generation has raised questions about authenticity in digital communication, blurred the lines between human and machine creativity, and challenged the way we approach tasks traditionally reserved for humans. This intense interest underscores a broader societal intrigue in generative AI's potential and its implications, setting the stage for a deep examination of the ethical, practical, and transformative impact of these technologies on organizations and society at large. Clearly, the potential implications of generative AI on organizations and society are wide-ranging. On the one hand, generative AI has the potential to greatly improve efficiency and productivity in various industries. For example, in the field of content creation, AI-generated content could help to significantly reduce the time and resources required to create high-quality content. Similarly, in the field of coding, AI-generated code could help to reduce the time and resources required to develop software. On the other hand, generative AI also raises a number of ethical and societal concerns. One concern is that it could lead to widespread job loss, as machines become capable of performing tasks that were previously done by humans. Additionally, there is also concern that AI-generated content could be used to spread misinformation or propaganda, as it becomes increasingly difficult to distinguish between human-generated and AI-generated content.

While generative AI is a rapidly advancing field that has the potential to greatly improve efficiency and productivity in various industries, it also raises many ethical and societal concerns. As this technology continues to evolve, it is important for organizations and society as a whole to consider the potential consequences and take proactive steps to address them. Additionally, many AI systems incorporate elements of multiple types of AI in order to perform their tasks. In addition, as "no-code" solutions for machine learning and deep learning become more prevalent, they are driving the evolution of AI platform types and blurring their boundaries. These platforms, referred to as "lightweight" forms of AI (Sundberg and Holmström (2022a, 2022b), allow for users with little or no coding experience to train models and reduce the gap between data experts and novice users. However, this also shifts the focus to domain expertise as a key factor in achieving complex AI objectives. As these platforms become integrated into larger systems, the distinctions between different types of AI will become less clear and decision-makers will need to consider the role of these platforms in their overall AI strategy.

The quality of data is critical for decision-making based on AI tools. AI tools use data to train models and make predictions, and the quality of the data used to train and test these models directly impacts the accuracy of the predictions made. Poor-quality data can lead to inaccurate or biased models, which can in turn lead to poor decision-making. Data quality can be defined as the degree to which data meets the requirements of its intended use. This includes factors such as accuracy, completeness, consistency, and timeliness. When data is of high quality, it is more likely to be fit for its intended use, and as a result, AI models trained on this data will be more accurate. On the other hand, low-quality data can lead to inaccurate or biased models, which can negatively impact decision-making.

One of the most common issues with data quality is bias. When datasets used to train AI models are not representative of the entire population, biases can occur. For instance, a credit risk assessment model trained predominantly on data from a specific ethnic group may develop biases that skew its predictions towards that group. Such a model may inaccurately assess individuals from other groups, potentially leading to unfair credit denials for those who might otherwise be deemed creditworthy. This lack of representativeness in the training data can compromise the model's decision-making effectiveness and fairness. Another issue with data quality is incompleteness. Data can be incomplete for a variety of reasons, such as missing data points or data that is not recorded. Incomplete data can lead to inaccurate predictions and poor decision-making. For example, if a model is trained on incomplete data to predict customer churn, it may not accurately predict when customers are likely to leave the organization, leading to poor decisions on how to retain customers.

Despite the vast amounts of data being generated in various forms, the advancements in analytical and data science frameworks are not keeping pace. Often, data science tasks are performed in an ad hoc manner by researchers who may not have a strong background in computer science or scalable data science, exacerbating the problem. Additionally, research data usually comprises information collected from multiple, disparate sources, necessitating significant integration and curation before it can be used effectively. This process is labor-intensive, often requiring substantial human involvement. The discovery, amalgamation, and curation of datasets, along with feature extraction, are all time-consuming yet crucial tasks for data scientists.

The phrase "data is the new oil" is often used to describe the relationship between data and value creation from AI because, like oil, data is a valuable resource that can be extracted, refined, and used to fuel various processes (see Alaimo & Kallinikos, 2022). It also emphasizes the importance of data as a raw material for AI systems and the need for organizations to invest in the collection and management of data to fuel their AI applications and create value. Interestingly, in the past couple of years, we have witnessed how digitalization in traditional industry settings is fundamentally changing how we understand and approach work and ways of knowing (Monteiro, 2022). The use of AI and automation in these settings can transform traditional work practices and decision-making by providing more efficient and accurate operations. For example, AI algorithms can be used to optimize production processes, predict maintenance needs, and improve the quality of products. Additionally, AI can help organizations make sense of the large amounts of data generated by their operations, allowing them to make better-informed decisions. As a result, the way we understand and approach work and knowledge in traditional industry settings is being transformed by digitalization and the integration of AI, and this shift has the potential to create significant value for organizations in these contexts.

Generative AI has moved the needle for what AI can and cannot do by expanding the capabilities of AI to generate new and original content such as text, images, and even code. This is a significant advancement as it allows AI to go beyond simply recognizing and processing data, but to actively create new data that can be used in a variety of applications. Additionally, with the advancements in generative AI, AI is also showing an increasing ability to understand and work with context. This means that while certain limitations of AI still exist, the increasing capabilities of generative AI are expanding the scope of what is possible for AI to achieve. As such, generative AI moves the boundary of what AI can and cannot do by expanding the capabilities of AI to generate new and original content such as text, images, and even code, and with the increasing ability to understand and work with context. This allows AI to be used in a wider range of applications and creates new possibilities for AI-generated content and insights.

The fact that AI is to be used in a wider range of applications demonstrates how AI research is a rapidly growing field with the potential to impact many aspects of our lives. However, the current dominant approach in AI research, which is computer science-centered, has limitations in fully addressing the complexity of the issues that AI raises. Transdisciplinary AI research, which involves collaboration between multiple disciplines, is important to fully understand and address the social, ethical, and economic implications of AI.

Traditionally, AI research has been dominated by computer science, which has included a focus on developing algorithms and technologies to improve the performance of AI systems. This approach has led to significant advancements in the field, such as the development of deep learning and the improvement of natural language processing. However, the computer science-centered approach has limitations in fully addressing the complex issues that AI raises. Clearly, AI has the potential to impact many aspects of our lives, such as employment, privacy, and decision-making. But these issues are not only technical in nature but also have social, ethical, and economic implications. Therefore, to fully understand and address these issues, it is important to involve perspectives from other disciplines, such as philosophy, sociology, and economics (for a discussion, see Lindgren & Holmström, 2020).

The social science perspective is particularly important in transdisciplinary AI research (Miller et al., 2017). Social scientists can provide insight into how AI systems are used and how they impact society (Gupta & Tu, 2020; Lindgren & Holmström, 2020). They can also help identify the potential biases and ethical issues that may arise in the development and deployment of AI systems. Indeed, social scientists and humanities scholars are beginning to take a more active role in AI research, recognizing that AI and social context are mutually shaping each other. AI technologies are not neutral; they are shaped by societal values, norms, and expectations, and at the same time, their development and use have a significant impact on society. Recognizing this complexity, an interdisciplinary approach is needed to fully understand and address the social and cultural implications of AI, and to ensure that the technology is developed and used in a responsible and ethical way.

AI has the potential to create significant value for organizations, but realizing this potential requires addressing several organizational and technical hurdles. A mutual shaping view, which recognizes that AI shapes organizations while organizations also shape AI, is important for addressing these hurdles (Lindgren & Holmström, 2020). The salient organizational and technical hurdles facing AI value creation in organizations must be approached through a mutual shaping view, recognizing that AI shapes organizations while organizations also shape AI.

On the organizational side, there are several hurdles that must be overcome to create value with AI. One of the most significant hurdles is the lack of understanding of AI among decision-makers. Many organizations are still trying to understand what AI is and how it can be used to create value (Feuerriegel et al., 2022). This can lead to a lack of buy-in and support for AI initiatives, as well as a lack of understanding of the potential benefits and limitations of AI. By recognizing that organizations shape AI, decision-makers and employees can be provided with the necessary knowledge and training to understand and effectively utilize AI. Another hurdle is the lack of a clear AI strategy. Without a clear strategy, organizations may struggle to identify the most valuable use cases for AI, or they may invest in AI projects that do not align with their overall business goals. The lack of a strategic vision and a grounded understanding of how AI can be used to create value, organizations may struggle to identify the right use cases and may not be able to effectively measure the success of their AI initiatives. By recognizing that AI shapes organizations, organizations can develop clear strategies and goals for AI implementation that consider the potential impact of AI on their operations and their competitive position. In addition, there is often a lack of data literacy and a shortage of skilled personnel who can manage and maintain the AI systems.

On the technical side, there are several hurdles that must be overcome as well. From a technical perspective, one of the main hurdles is the lack of data and computational resources. Without sufficient data and computational resources, organizations may struggle to train and deploy AI models. By recognizing that organizations shape AI, organizations can invest in data and computational resources to support their AI initiatives. A related hurdle is the quality of data. AI systems rely on data to train models and make predictions, and the quality of the data used to train and test these models directly impacts the accuracy of the predictions made. Poor-quality data can lead to inaccurate or biased models, which can in turn lead to poor decision-making. Another technical hurdle is the lack of understanding of the technical aspects of AI, such as machine learning algorithms and architectures. By recognizing that organizations shape AI, organizations can invest in the necessary technical expertise to support their AI initiatives. Yet another hurdle is the interpretability and explainability of AI systems. AI systems can be opaque and difficult to understand, making it hard for decision-makers to trust the predictions made by these systems.

To overcome these hurdles – the organizational and the technical – organizations need to approach AI through a mutual shaping view. This means recognizing that AI shapes organizations while organizations also shape AI. Organizations need to shape AI by developing a clear strategy, investing in data literacy and skilled personnel, and addressing issues of interpretability and explainability. As such, the salient organizational and technical hurdles facing AI value creation in organizations must be approached through a mutual shaping view, recognizing that AI shapes organizations while organizations also shape AI. This approach allows organizations to understand the potential impact of AI on their operations and competitive position, and to invest in the necessary knowledge, strategies, data, computational resources, and technical expertise to support their AI initiatives.

In the context of AI and management, organizations face interconnected challenges that impact the delegation of decisions to AI systems. These challenges span the roles of managers, the decision-making process, and the broader organizational structure. Elaborating on this, we next discuss three salient organizational and technical hurdles facing AI in the delegation of management decisions, how they are intertwined, and show potential solutions to overcome them. These hurdles cover (1) the managerial role, (2) the decision-making process, and its relationship with (3) the organization.

The managerial role: With AI's growing capability to make autonomous decisions, managers might question their position and become reluctant to cede decision-making power to machines. As such, as AI's ability to make autonomous decisions is expanding, it is imperative to address the concerns of managers who may feel their role is being encroached upon. The integration of AI into decision-making processes can indeed alter managerial roles, but it also offers opportunities to enhance these roles:

- ***Education and training:*** Equip managers with a deep understanding of AI's capabilities to foster confidence in using AI as a decision-support tool rather than a replacement.
- ***Participatory design:*** Involve managers in the development of AI systems to ensure their insights contribute to AI decision-making frameworks.
- ***Role redefinition:*** Realign managerial roles to focus on tasks that AI cannot perform, such as empathy-driven leadership and complex problem-solving.

Decision-making process: The intricacy of AI algorithms often results in a lack of clarity about how decisions are made, leading to concerns over transparency and accountability. When integrating AI into decision-making processes, the opaqueness of AI algorithms can raise concerns about transparency and accountability. To address these issues, organizations can explore the following potential solutions:

- ***Explainable AI:*** Invest in AI systems that offer explanations for their reasoning and outcomes, making their decision-making process more transparent.
- ***Human-AI collaboration:*** Establish protocols where AI decisions are subject to human review, especially in high-stakes scenarios, to align AI outputs with organizational goals and ethical standards.

The organization: The integration of AI into management decisions has significant implications for organizational dynamics and structures. The integration of AI into management decisions can indeed reshape the dynamics and structures within an organization. To leverage AI effectively while maintaining a harmonious organizational environment, consider the following potential solutions:

- ***Inclusive development:*** Engage diverse employee groups in the AI integration process to align the technology with the organization's culture and values.

Policy development: Formulate clear policies regarding AI use to guide ethical and responsible application and to clarify how AI-driven decisions are made.

Change management: Implement comprehensive change management strategies to facilitate the adaptation of employees to new AI-based procedures and to foster an AI-ready culture.

Addressing these hurdles requires a multifaceted approach that combines technological solutions with strategic human resource management and organizational development. It also requires an integration of AI into management decision-making and a comprehensive understanding of the complex and interrelated challenges that organizations face. The hurdles in redefining managerial roles, restructuring the decision-making process, and aligning it with organizational objectives highlight the intricate balance needed between human oversight and AI efficiency. By examining the specific organizational and technical obstacles and exploring practical solutions, organizations can better address these hurdles. Ultimately, the successful delegation of decisions to AI systems hinges on harmonizing these elements to foster an environment where AI can augment human capabilities while maintaining accountability and strategic alignment. By succeeding in doing so, organizations can leverage AI to enhance decision-making, streamline operations, and drive innovation, all while ensuring that the human aspect of management is not only preserved but also augmented.

Figure 1.1 depicts three interrelated dimensions of AI-related value creation within organizations: decision-making processes, managerial roles, and the organization. The decision-making processes dimension concerns how AI is integrated into organizational decision-making, highlighting the need for transparent and accountable algorithmic support in managerial decisions. The managerial roles dimension addresses the evolving responsibilities of managers as AI systems augment or automate certain tasks; rather than rendering managers obsolete, AI shifts their focus towards oversight, strategic guidance, and other functions that leverage uniquely human judgment. The organization dimension encompasses the structural and cultural context needed to support AI integration, emphasizing that supportive policies, inclusive practices, and effective change management are essential to align AI initiatives with the organization's goals and values. Depicting these elements as slices of a pie chart underscores that each dimension is an integral part of a larger whole – all three must work in concert for AI to effectively generate and sustain organizational value.

Taken together, these three dimensions provide a conceptual foundation for analyzing how organizations make sense of AI and derive tangible value from it. This integrated perspective ensures that any examination of AI in business remains grounded in organizational reality: realizing AI's potential is not purely a technical matter but a socio-technical process requiring concurrent

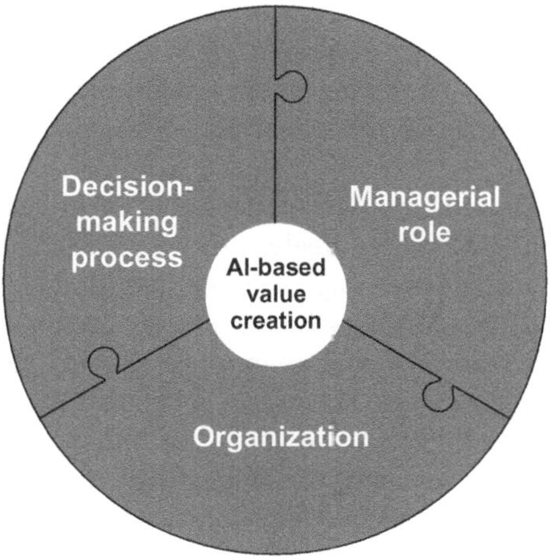

Figure 1.1 Key dimensions in AI-related value creation in organizations

adjustments in decision practices, managerial approaches, and organizational structures. Building on this foundation, the discussion now turns to the broader context beyond the single firm, exploring how these internal factors interact with wider ecosystems and collaborative networks to further enhance AI-driven value creation.

While AI has emerged as a transformative driver of innovation and competitive advantage across industries, organizations often struggle to translate AI's technical potential into tangible business value when it is pursued in isolation. A growing recognition in both industry and research is that AI's true potential is realized not within single firms, but in the context of broader networks of collaboration. In today's interconnected economy, firms leverage AI more effectively by engaging with an ecosystem of partners, suppliers, customers, and complementary innovators, rather than working alone. Viewing AI through an ecosystem lens underscores that value creation is no longer the domain of one company, but a shared endeavor among many interdependent actors.

Adopting an AI ecosystem approach means recognizing that innovation and competitive advantage emerge from complex, cross-organizational systems rather than isolated corporate efforts. Companies now operate as part of dynamic ecosystems in which multiple stakeholders co-evolve and co-create solutions. In such environments, AI initiatives benefit from diverse contributions – one participant might provide data, another algorithms, and others domain expertise or market access. This collaborative model of joint value creation ensures that the outcomes of AI deployments are richer and more robust than any single actor could achieve alone. It builds on open innovation principles, where knowledge and resources flow across firm boundaries to spark new ideas and opportunities. By pooling complementary capabilities, an AI ecosystem can tackle complex challenges and unlock synergies that remain out of reach when organizations act solely within their own silos. The ecosystem perspective thus offers a more comprehensive understanding of how AI-driven innovation unfolds, highlighting that the success of one player's AI solution often depends on the contributions of many others in the network.

When AI is developed and deployed within a well-orchestrated ecosystem, several advantages become clear. Data flows more freely across organizational boundaries, as ecosystem partners share data and insights to improve AI models and decision-making. This access to diverse, high-quality data (often from multiple industries or user groups) can dramatically enhance machine learning performance and the relevance of AI-driven services. Ecosystem collaboration also enables the development of dynamic capabilities – the ability for firms to rapidly sense market changes, learn from partners, and reconfigure their resources and algorithms in response. Because participants coordinate their efforts (often through shared digital platforms), they can integrate AI solutions seamlessly, ensuring interoperability of tools and technologies across the network. Such platform-based coordination provides a foundation for scaling AI applications: successful innovations can be rolled out across the ecosystem's many partners and markets far more quickly than a single firm could achieve. Moreover, the ecosystem's collective capacity fosters continuous improvement; as each actor experiments and adapts, the lessons and improvements circulate to others. In sum, deploying AI in an ecosystem accelerates innovation, amplifies learning, and creates value that is distributed among the collaborators – with feedback loops that make the whole network increasingly intelligent and effective over time.

Despite these potential benefits, managers and policymakers currently face a gap in understanding how to strategically harness AI within an ecosystem context. Most traditional AI deployment strategies focus on firm-level implementation and do not address the challenges of coordinating across multiple organizations. As a result, companies may struggle with issues of scaling, interoperability, and sustained value creation in their AI initiatives. For example, an AI solution proven in one organization may fail to scale if partners cannot easily adopt or integrate it, and data-sharing barriers or misaligned incentives can stall ecosystem-wide adoption. Interoperability challenges arise when proprietary systems cannot seamlessly connect, underscoring the need for common platforms or standards to support AI collaboration. Furthermore, creating sustained value from AI requires ongoing adaptation and contribution from many players, which is difficult when firms view AI projects in isolation rather than as part of a living, evolving network. These issues highlight why a shift in management thinking is needed: capturing AI's full value calls for joint orchestration of innovation across an ecosystem, not just within a single enterprise. However, clear guidance on how to manage AI-powered innovation in an ecosystem setting remains limited. This lack of frameworks and models means that practitioners are often unsure how to build the partnerships, governance structures, and shared resources necessary for AI ecosystems to thrive. As a result, many AI initiatives underperform or remain trapped in pilot stages, never realizing the transformative impact that a coordinated ecosystem approach can achieve.

This paper responds to these challenges by examining how an ecosystem approach can unlock new pathways for creating value from AI. It builds conceptually on emerging insights from digital business ecosystems and management theory, positing that firms must move beyond standalone AI adoption towards strategies that emphasize joint value co-creation, data sharing, platform-based coordination, and collective dynamic capabilities development. In doing so, the discussion remains general (without focusing on any single company or case) to extract broadly applicable principles for academics, practitioners, and policymakers. The aim is to deepen managerial understanding of how AI-enabled innovation and transformation occur within ecosystem contexts, thereby filling current gaps in guidance for strategic decision-making. Ultimately, we position the ecosystem approach as a strategic response to the practical challenges of scaling AI solutions, ensuring interoperability among diverse stakeholders, and sustaining value creation over time. By viewing AI through an ecosystem lens, leaders can better navigate the complexities of digital transformation and collaboratively harness AI's transformative potential for competitive advantage and societal benefit.

While Hubert Dreyfus argued that AI has limitations and that it will never be able to fully replicate human intelligence (Dreyfus, 1972), it is important to note that AI obviously has made significant progress since the book was first published in 1972. One limitation that Dreyfus pointed out is that AI lacks the ability to understand context and common sense. However, recent advancements in AI, such as deep learning and neural networks, have allowed computers to process large amounts of data and have improved their ability to understand context. Another limitation that Dreyfus mentioned is that AI lacks the ability to make judgments and decisions based on ethical considerations. However, recent research in AI ethics has begun to address this issue (e.g. Villegas-Galaviz & Martin, 2023). Despite these limitations, AI has been able to perform tasks that were once thought to be exclusively human, such as playing chess at a grandmaster level and beating strong human players. It is likely that in the next few years, generative AI will continue to push the boundaries of what AI can do. As such, while AI has limitations that prevent it from fully replicating human intelligence, it has made significant progress in recent years and is likely to continue to do so in the future.

AI's trajectory from a fledgling concept to a cornerstone of modern society illustrates a remarkable evolution, reflecting impressive improvements in capabilities and applications. Since its inception, AI has undergone several waves of optimism and skepticism, yet each wave has left behind a trail of progress. In the early days, AI's capabilities were limited to basic tasks and simple games, like chess, which essentially were narrow in scope. From those foundations, we have witnessed a rapid acceleration, particularly in the last two decades. This acceleration can be attributed to exponential increases in computational power, advancements in machine learning algorithms, and the availability of massive datasets.

Today, AI's reach has extended far beyond the initial academic world into practical, everyday applications. Considering that we now have AI that can drive cars, create art, write text, and even make complex financial decisions, this is clearly a far cry from the simple problem-solving programs of the 1950s and 1960s. Now, AI systems can learn from data, improve over time, and perform tasks that were once thought to be the exclusive domain of human intelligence. Moreover, AI's ability to process and analyze large volumes of data has led to groundbreaking discoveries in fields such as healthcare, where it aids in disease diagnosis and personalized medicine. In business, AI has become increasingly indispensable for organizations looking to gain insights from data analytics, automate processes, and enhance customer experiences.

As AI continues to develop, it is not just the capabilities that are changing; it is also the very nature of what AI can be. With the advent of neural networks and deep learning, AI can now engage in tasks involving perception and decision-making in complex, unstructured environments. This represents a shift from AI as a tool for automating tasks to AI as an agent capable of learning, adapting, and potentially working collaboratively with humans. Having said this, we also need to consider how AI's rapid evolution also brings about significant ethical, economic, and social considerations that must be addressed. As AI becomes more ingrained in society, the line between what AI can do and what it should do becomes increasingly important to consider. The future of AI, therefore, is not just a question of technological capability but also of the choices we make about its application and integration into the fabric of our daily lives.

A key for managing AI effectively is to manage AI by addressing the key challenges associated with AI management, and to foster a culture of continuous learning and collaboration around AI. By doing so, organizations can harness the full potential of generative AI, unlocking value creation and achieving sustainable growth in an increasingly competitive AI landscape. In this context, value creation through AI represents a transformative concept in the context of organizational growth and innovation. It refers to the potential of AI to catalyze a level of value generation that surpasses traditional incremental improvements and marginal enhancements. This form of value creation is termed radical because it suggests that the benefits AI can offer are not confined by conventional limitations or linear growth trajectories. Instead, AI can propel organizations to pursue efficiency, innovation, and market leadership.

When effectively leveraged, AI can lead to the development of innovative products, services, and business models that were previously unattainable. For example, AI-driven analytics can identify new market opportunities or customer segments by discerning patterns invisible to human analysts. AI can also automate complex processes, from manufacturing to customer service, reducing costs and improving service quality simultaneously. Moreover, AI's ability to generate deep insights can lead to significant enhancements in decision-making processes. These insights can help organizations reduce waste, optimize operations, and tailor their offerings to meet the precise needs of their customers. However, value creation is not automatic; it requires strategic management and a conducive organizational environment. Organizations must ensure they have robust data governance frameworks to feed accurate and high-quality data into AI systems. They also need to foster a culture that embraces change and innovation, where stakeholders are prepared to rethink traditional business models and processes in light of AI's capabilities. Furthermore, ethical considerations and potential risks associated with AI, such as privacy concerns, bias, and job displacement, must be carefully managed. Organizations need to deploy AI responsibly, ensuring transparency, fairness, and accountability in AI systems to sustain trust and avoid societal backlash.

To create value from AI by adopting an ecosystem view offers a vision of what organizations can achieve when they harness the transformative power of AI technologies. By embracing AI's core attributes of adaptability, scalability, and the ability to facilitate external collaborations, organizations can break through previous limitations and unlock exponential benefits. However, realizing this potential requires thoughtful strategy, careful management, and a commitment to ethical practices, ensuring that AI is used not just for economic gains but also in a manner that benefits society at large.

Creating value from AI by adopting an ecosystem view refers to the potential for AI technologies to generate significant and continuous value not only across various aspects of an organization but also beyond organizational boundaries, surpassing what we have learned to be traditional growth limitations and unlocking new opportunities for innovation, efficiency, and competitive advantage. As such, value creation in AI arises from its unique properties, such as adaptability, scalability, and its ability to facilitate external collaborations and network effects. It should be obvious that value creation in AI is not guaranteed but rather depends on effective AI management and collaboration between AI experts and domain experts within organizations. By doing just that, organizations can unlock value creation, achieving sustainable growth and maintaining a competitive edge in the rapidly evolving AI landscape.

AI, jobs, and skills

Exploring the potential for AI technologies to generate significant and continuous value within and across organizations opens up new opportunities for innovation, efficiency, and competitive advantage. But a side effect that is problematic and must be considered is the ways in which AI is likely to have a significant impact on jobs and skills in organizations. While there is much debate about the potential effects of AI on the labor market, it is generally agreed that it may lead to both job displacement and job creation (Frey & Osborne, 2017). It seems evident that AI is rapidly transforming the way we live and work, and it has demonstrated the potential to automate many tasks that were previously performed by humans, leading to job displacement (Brynjolfsson & McAfee, 2014). However, it also has the potential to create new jobs and improve the productivity of existing ones. Against this backdrop, it is important to explore in more detail the role AI may play in job displacement and job creation.

AI is clearly a potentially transformative technology. This transformation through AI is particularly evident in how it reshapes industries, fostering new business models that leverage predictive insights for strategic advantage. Each leap forward with AI paves the way for systems that are not only automated but also inherently adaptive, capable of evolving with changing data and objectives. However, history tells us that transformation does not come easy. While the initial fruits of a new technology are point applications, real transformation comes when new socio-technical systems that are driven by the technology are created.

But such a transformation may also be disruptive. By disruptive, we mean that it changes the roles of many people and organizations and, alongside those changes, causes shifts in power. That is, there are likely to be economic winners and losers, especially if system change occurs relatively quickly. The term disruption emerged from the work of Clayton Christensen. Christensen noted that incumbent firms can find themselves "asking the wrong questions" regarding new technologies and their value to customers (Christensen, 2013). Thus, they shy away from certain technologies that offer few advantages to their own customers. By contrast, those very same technologies appeal to customers who are either not served or underserved by existing market leaders. The disruption caused by AI is a prime example of Christensen's theory in action. Industries that have traditionally relied on human expertise are increasingly being challenged by AI systems capable of not only matching but often surpassing human performance in specific tasks. This technological shift can radically alter market dynamics, as organizations that adopt AI may gain a significant competitive edge. These firms can harness AI to cater to new markets or to serve existing ones more efficiently, potentially capturing a larger market share. Moreover, the disruptive nature of AI extends beyond market competition. It also affects the workforce as roles that once required human decision-making are increasingly automated. This can lead to a realignment of job requirements, with a higher emphasis on AI oversight and management rather than on routine execution. While some jobs may be rendered obsolete, new opportunities emerge in the fields of AI maintenance, development, and ethical governance.

In the wake of AI adoption in an industry, the imbalance in AI adoption between firms can lead to what Christensen refers to as the "innovator's dilemma," where established market leaders may hesitate to embrace new technologies due to their investment in the status quo. This hesitation can be detrimental, as it allows smaller, more agile firms to capitalize on the efficiencies and capabilities that AI offers. We have already seen that the ingredients for such blind spots with respect to AI lie in underestimating AI's potential in different contexts, and how many incumbent firms are "stuck" in traditional modes of thinking. When this happens, managing disruption is not simply about targeting a different set of customers but instead about reformulating the organization of businesses and the problems that need to be their priorities. This underestimation of AI's potential can lead to significant strategic oversights. For example, AI's ability to analyze and interpret vast quantities of data can uncover insights that fundamentally challenge existing business assumptions. These insights can redefine what constitutes value in a given industry and can introduce new metrics for success. As a result, businesses may need to shift their focus from solely improving existing products and services to also pioneering innovative solutions that were previously unfeasible or unseen in the market.

Incorporating AI into business strategy necessitates a reevaluation of an organization's structure and goals. AI does not merely support existing processes – it often necessitates the creation of new roles, teams, and divisions dedicated to data science, AI ethics, and continuous technological innovation. Moreover, AI's predictive capabilities and potential for personalization mean that organizations must rethink their customer engagement strategies, moving towards more dynamic, responsive, and individualized interactions. Furthermore, AI's implications extend to the core of organizational problem-solving. The traditional approach of incrementally improving products may give way to a paradigm where the challenge is to fundamentally reimagine products using AI's capabilities. This could involve harnessing AI to create more sustainable operations, to develop products that adapt over time to user needs, or to provide services that anticipate consumer demands before they are explicitly expressed.

The organizations that succeed in this new era will likely be those that view AI not as a tool but as a catalyst for redefining their business models. These organizations will prioritize agility and foster a culture of innovation that embraces experimentation. Additionally, they will invest in upskilling their workforce to handle the sophisticated demands of AI technologies and commit to the responsible use of AI, ensuring that ethical considerations are integral to their deployment of AI. Thus, the management of AI-driven disruption lies not just in adapting to change but in leading it. It is about recognizing that AI can redefine not only how businesses operate but also what they aim to achieve. It is about having the vision to see beyond the horizon guided by the transformative potential of artificial intelligence.

The advent of AI presents a dual-edged sword in the labor market. On the one hand, it has the potential to render certain jobs redundant, particularly where routine or repetitive tasks are prevalent. The McKinsey Global Institute projects that by 2030, automation spurred by AI could affect up to 800 million jobs globally. This impact is anticipated to be felt most acutely in sectors such as transportation, manufacturing, and retail. On the other hand, AI's rise is not a mere harbinger of job loss but a catalyst for job evolution. It is poised to create a surge in demand for new skill sets, particularly in domains like data science and machine learning. By taking over monotonous tasks, AI liberates the human workforce to pursue more creative and strategic endeavors, potentially boosting productivity and birthing entirely new job categories.

Furthermore, AI's capacity to enhance human abilities may pave the way for new job types and new methodologies of work. It holds promise for refining decision-making, streamlining operations, and propelling innovation, which in turn could lead to new business models, as well as novel products and services. A quintessential example of this is in healthcare, where AI is projected to introduce new roles such as data analysts and AI-powered medical assistants. Moreover, AI could democratize work opportunities, fostering more inclusive work environments. With its ability to support remote work structures, AI could significantly increase workforce participation among traditionally underrepresented groups, such as individuals with disabilities, the elderly, and women, by offering more adaptable and accessible work conditions.

AI's impact on jobs will, without a doubt, lead to AI displacing some jobs, and simultaneously seeding the labor market with new opportunities, redefining roles and enhancing human capabilities, which could lead to a more inclusive and innovative future workforce. In addition, AI's impact on jobs will differ across sectors, regions, and skill levels, making it vital for organizations and governments to proactively address the challenges and opportunities AI presents for employment. Investing in reskilling and upskilling programs is essential. AI is likely to displace jobs involving repetitive, routine, or predictable tasks, as these tasks are easily automated. With AI's increasing sophistication, it can perform these tasks more efficiently and accurately than humans, potentially leading to job losses in industries like manufacturing, transportation, and customer service. However, AI is also expected to create new jobs in areas such as data analysis, machine learning, and AI development, as demand for individuals skilled in developing, implementing, and maintaining AI systems grows.

AI's impact on required job skills is another important aspect to consider. As AI performs tasks previously needing specialized skills, such as data analysis and decision-making, the demand for those skills may decrease. However, this could increase demand for skills in data interpretation, problem-solving, and strategic thinking. Considering AI's impact on work nature, automating repetitive tasks allows employees to focus on higher-value tasks requiring human skills like creativity, critical thinking, and emotional intelligence. This may shift job demand towards roles that require these human skills. It should be clear that AI has the potential to both displace and create jobs. While the risk of job displacement is real, it is important to recognize that AI also has the potential to improve productivity, create new jobs, and augment human capabilities in ways that lead to new ways of working. Organizations and governments must be proactive in addressing the challenges and opportunities that AI presents in terms of work. It should be noted that the debate on AI and job displacement today has its precursor in the discussions of the 1970s and 1980s, when scholars discussed in detail how new technology affected jobs and the quality of working life (e.g. Ehn, 1988). In this research, it was argued that new technology, such as automation and computerization, had a significant impact on the structure of work and the nature of jobs. It was demonstrated how the new technologies introduced in the 1970s and 1980s led to the displacement of jobs that involved repetitive, routine, or predictable tasks and the creation of new jobs that required new skills and knowledge. It was also demonstrated how new technology had a significant impact on the quality of working life. In the book by Ehn (1988), it was argued that the introduction of new technology led to a shift in the types of jobs that were in demand, with an emphasis on jobs that required higher-level skills and knowledge. It was also argued that new technology led to a change in the nature of work itself, with an increased focus on problem-solving, critical thinking, and decision-making.

The work on the impact of new technology on work and working life from the 1970s and 1980s is particularly relevant to the current debate on AI and job displacement. As AI becomes more widely adopted, it is likely to have a significant impact on jobs and skills in organizations, similar to the impact of new technology in the 1970s and 1980s. As AI becomes more widely adopted, it is likely to have a significant impact on jobs and skills in organizations. While it will lead to job displacement in some areas, it will also lead to the creation of new jobs in other areas, and a deeper understanding of such changes requires consideration of the key and interconnected dimensions in AI-related value creation in organizations: the organization, the decision-making process, and the managerial role. In light of the historical context provided by the impact of new technology on work in the 1970s and 1980s, it is crucial to recognize that the influence of AI on job displacement and creation is not a predetermined outcome. Instead, it is a dynamic process that requires active and informed decision-making, and we need to raise our voices and discuss what kind of society we ideally would like to see. To accomplish this, we must consider the intertwined aspects of organizational structure, decision-making processes, and managerial roles. By proactively engaging with these dimensions, we can shape the societal and economic impacts of AI, steering them towards outcomes that align with our values and desired societal structure. This necessitates a deliberate effort to ensure that the integration of AI fosters job growth, enhances skills, and promotes equitable opportunities across the workforce.

AI and value creation

Traditionally, an organization's value proposition has been seen as fairly constant over time. Products may be updated, marketing campaigns refreshed, or operations improved, but the basic value a business offered to its customers was assumed to be relatively constant. Under such circumstances, a successful business was one that had a clear value proposition, found a point of market differentiation (e.g. price or branding), and focused on executing and delivering the best version of the same value proposition to its customers year after year.

In the AI age, relying on an unchanging value proposition is inviting challenge and eventual disruption by new competitors. Although industries will vary as to the exact timing and nature of their transformation by new AI technologies, those who assume it will be a little farther down the road are most likely to be run over. The only sure response to a shifting business environment is to take a path of constant evolution, looking to every technology as a way to extend and improve our value proposition to our customers.

The relationship between technology and value creation is a fascinating and ever-evolving topic. Value creation from an ecosystem view refers to the idea that the value generated by a technology or solution can expand rapidly beyond the initial task, eventually impacting the entire organization and even transcending its boundaries. When it comes to value creation for organizations, AI possesses a potential that can truly be termed as radical. This is due to a multitude of factors unique to AI that together lead to an exponential increase in opportunities for businesses across sectors. First, AI is inherently scalable. It can process vast amounts of data and generate insights or create outputs much more efficiently than humans, potentially leading to massive productivity gains and cost savings. For instance, AI can streamline supply chains by predicting demand trends, or it can enhance customer service by powering chatbots that handle routine queries round-the-clock. Second, AI can learn and improve autonomously. Given enough data and computational power, it can identify patterns, make predictions, and even create new content with minimal human intervention. This ability to "learn" enables AI to continuously adapt and improve, thereby constantly creating new value. Third, the versatility of AI applications is staggering. From healthcare to finance to entertainment, AI can add value in diverse ways in virtually every sector. It can generate personalized recommendations for customers, assist doctors in diagnosing diseases, automate accounting tasks, create new music or art, and much more.

Moreover, the innovative applications of AI can lead to the creation of entirely new products, services, and business models, opening up novel revenue streams. For instance, many organizations are already leveraging AI to offer personalized digital content, predictive maintenance services, and AI-powered software solutions. Another important aspect is the ability of AI to "amplify" human capabilities. By automating routine tasks and generating insights from data, AI can free up humans to focus on tasks that require creativity, critical thinking, and emotional intelligence. This can lead to improved decision-making, innovation, and customer relationships, which in turn create substantial value. Finally, as AI technologies continue to advance, they will unlock even more possibilities for value creation. Innovations in AI research and increasing computational power will lead to AI systems that are more capable, efficient, and versatile. In particular, advances in areas like natural language understanding and reinforcement learning could revolutionize how AI is used in business. As such, AI offers a pathway to value creation for organizations. It can create value in ways we can currently envision, but perhaps more importantly, it also holds the potential to create value in ways we cannot even imagine yet.

AI has the potential to trigger such value creation in various ways:

Adaptability: AI models can learn and adapt to new information and situations, making them highly versatile. This adaptability means that AI can be deployed for various tasks and can evolve to meet changing organizational needs, leading to continuous value creation and organizational growth.

Scalability: AI models can process and analyze vast amounts of data, enabling them to identify patterns, trends, and insights that might be missed by human analysts. This ability to scale allows organizations to leverage AI for a wide range of tasks, from simple automation to more complex problem-solving.

External collaborations: AI can also enable organizations to collaborate more effectively with external partners, such as suppliers, customers, and other stakeholders. By streamlining communication and data exchange, AI can help create new business opportunities and drive value creation beyond the organization's boundaries.

Network effects: As AI becomes more integrated into various aspects of an organization, its value will continue to grow exponentially. This growth can lead to a positive feedback loop, where the increased value generated by AI attracts more resources, investment, and talent, further fueling the cycle of value creation.

AI has seen immense evolution over the past few decades, which has changed its role and perception from being an organizational tool to a generative resource (see Table 1.1). In the early days of AI, its usage was largely confined to individual organizations. In the Organizational View, AI was seen as an organizational asset. The focus was on using AI to improve efficiencies, automate processes, and enhance decision-making within the boundaries of the organization. Examples of this use include the use of rule-based systems in expert systems, AI for optimizing logistics in supply chain management, and machine learning for predictive analytics. During this phase, AI's primary role was to serve as an internal resource that could enhance a company's competitive edge by improving its operations, making its processes more efficient, and providing insightful data analysis.

As technology advanced, so did the way organizations interact with AI. In this second phase – the Relational View – AI started serving as a resource between organizations, facilitating interaction and cooperation. For example, organizations began to share AI models and insights to collectively benefit from AI advancements. AI also started playing a role in creating strategic alliances, fostering innovation, and promoting knowledge sharing between organizations. New marketplaces, where organizations could buy, sell, or share AI models, started to emerge during this period. In this phase, the focus was on mutual benefits and shared growth.

In the third and most recent phase – the Ecosystem View – the rise of advanced AI models, along with the rapid growth of decentralized and distributed technologies, have led to an ecosystem view of AI. Here, the boundaries of AI usage are no longer limited by organizational or relational boundaries. Generative AI models, capable of creating human-like text, designs, music, and more, are openly available for anyone to utilize, regardless of their organizational affiliation. This democratization of AI technology has led to the emergence of new use cases that were previously unimaginable. AI can now be seen as a universally available resource, powering a wide range of applications from personal AI tutors to advanced research tools. This has also led to new societal and ethical considerations, as the impact of AI now extends well beyond the boundaries of any one organization. In this view, the role of AI has evolved from being a strategic resource for competitive advantage to a societal resource with the potential to reshape our world in profound ways.

Each of these phases represents an increasingly sophisticated level of AI integration within businesses and society, with corresponding changes in the context, the role of technology and the organization, data resources, and key value creation challenges. The evolution of AI from an Organizational View to a Relational View, and towards the Ecosystem View, marks a paradigm shift in how we perceive and use this technology. While initially seen as a tool for operational efficiency, AI has gradually become a critical part of inter-organizational relationships and is now envisioned as a vital component of societal ecosystems. With each phase, the role of technology, organizations, data resources, and value creation challenges has morphed, reflecting AI's increasing complexity and broadening scope. As we move towards the Ecosystem View of AI, it becomes essential to address the accompanying challenges to fully realize AI's potential in creating a better future.

In the coming years, AI is likely to trigger several types of value creation, and each type of value creation is likely to evolve as generative AI models evolve and improve. First, related to adaptability, we will in the coming years witness how generative AI models continue to improve; their ability to learn and adapt to new information and situations will become even more sophisticated. This adaptability will enable organizations to use AI for a broader range of tasks, including those that require advanced problem-solving and decision-making capabilities. This continuous evolution will lead to the creation of innovative products, services, and solutions that can address emerging challenges and capitalize on new opportunities, driving sustained value creation and organizational growth. Second, related to scalability, the scalability of generative AI models will continue to advance, allowing organizations to process and analyze increasingly large and complex datasets. As AI systems become more capable

Table 1.1 Three views on AI

	Organizational view	**Relational view**	**Ecosystem view**
Context	Hierarchy	Bilateral relationships	Ecosystem
Role of technology	Supporting	Stretching	Generative
Role of focal organization	Owner and curator of data resources	Party to a bilateral agreement establishing conditions for combining data across organizational boundaries	Participant or orchestrator of an ecosystem collecting data resources from a variety of sources
Data resources	Complementary organization-specific data resources combined from different data sets	Complementary data resources from different organizations combined on the basis of bilateral agreements	Complementary data resources collected from ecosystem
Key value creation challenges	Developing capabilities to collect, integrate, analyze, and exploit data resources	Negotiating legal, technical and competitive issues regarding data collection, data analysis, and value creation	Developing boundary resources to coordinate data collection, data analysis, and value creation

of handling big data, they will provide deeper insights and more accurate predictions, leading to better decision-making and more informed strategies. This enhanced scalability will enable organizations to create value across multiple functions, from optimizing operations and reducing costs to identifying new market opportunities and driving revenue growth. Third, with regard to external collaborations, organizations will increasingly leverage AI-driven technologies to facilitate external collaborations as generative AI becomes more widespread and accessible. AI can help streamline communication, data exchange, and decision-making processes among stakeholders, making it easier for organizations to form strategic partnerships and alliances. These collaborations can lead to the development of new business models, shared innovations, and joint ventures, driving value creation beyond the organization's boundaries and fostering a more interconnected and collaborative business ecosystem. Fourth, related to network effects, we will witness how AI becomes more deeply integrated into various aspects of organizations in the coming years and, as a consequence, its value will continue to grow exponentially due to network effects. The increased value generated by AI will attract more resources, investment, and talent, further fueling the cycle of value creation. This positive feedback loop will lead to the development of more advanced AI technologies and applications, which in turn will drive additional value creation and reinforce the organization's competitive advantage. Moreover, as AI adoption becomes more widespread, the benefits of AI will extend beyond individual organizations to entire industries and economies, creating a more efficient, innovative, and resilient global business landscape.

AI is not merely an addition to organizational practice; it is an integral part of it. AI's capabilities deeply influence the structural, strategic, and operational facets of an organization. It shapes how strategies are formulated, decisions are made, and organizations evolve. The interdependence between AI and organizational practices signifies that when organizations reshape their practices around AI, they not only automate existing processes but also create new avenues for innovation and strategic advantage. This symbiotic relationship sets the stage for transformative changes across the organizational spectrum, laying the groundwork for generative AI to effectively drive growth and value creation.

While AI's transformative potential is undeniable, it necessitates a strategic approach to adoption – one that extends beyond the confines of the "AI experimentation trap." To actualize AI's value-creation capabilities, organizations must transcend the lure of experimentation for its own sake. Avoiding this trap is a necessary but insufficient condition for building value from AI; it is the foundational step upon which sustainable integration of AI into organizational practices must be built. As organizations move past experimentation, they must focus on embedding AI into the decision-making fabric of the company, fostering an AI-augmented culture that promotes continuous learning and innovation. This involves a shift from isolated AI projects to a comprehensive strategy where AI becomes a core driver of business processes, competitive strategy, and organizational adaptability By doing so, they leverage AI not just as a tool for incremental improvement, but as a catalyst for reinvention and long-term value creation.

The coming years will see AI triggering value creation through enhanced adaptability, scalability, external collaborations, and network effects. By harnessing these capabilities, organizations can unlock the full potential of generative AI and achieve sustainable growth in an increasingly competitive landscape. Clearly, generative AI has the potential to trigger value creation by scaling and adapting to different tasks, enabling customization, enhancing decision-making, fostering cross-functional collaboration, and facilitating external partnerships. As AI continues to advance and become more integrated into organizational processes, its potential to drive value creation will only grow. However, organizations must also be aware of the ethical considerations and potential risks associated with AI deployment to ensure that this value is generated responsibly and sustainably.

Chapter 2

Leveraging AI and data work for value creation

AI, automation, and augmentation

AI has quickly moved from being a novel technology to a core component of many organizations. However, achieving this potential is not straightforward – the road to value creation is not always easy to find. One reason for this is that AI's success depends fundamentally on data. Data is the raw material that fuels algorithms and insights. An organization's ability to collect, process, store, and analyze data largely determines the success of its AI initiatives. Accordingly, data work has ascended to a key function in today's AI-powered organizations. In practice, data work encompasses a range of activities from ensuring data quality and governance to developing data models that can predict, optimize, and automate processes. Organizations are increasingly investing in robust data infrastructures, adopting data-centric mindsets, and making efforts to cultivate skills in data science and analytics. These steps are imperative not only to operate current AI systems but also to pave the way for more advanced AI applications in the future. Moreover, as the scope of AI expands, data's role becomes even more strategic. It underpins decision-making, drives customer insights, and optimizes operations. Companies that harness their data effectively will be at the forefront of innovation – able to anticipate market trends, personalize customer experiences, and respond dynamically to change. In short, investing in data work is not just a technical necessity but a strategic imperative for organizations aiming to fully leverage the transformative power of AI.

In today's organizations, AI applications generally fall along a spectrum between automation and augmentation. Automation uses AI to perform tasks independently, potentially replacing the need for human involvement. This can bring improved efficiency and cost savings, but automation has limitations: AI systems often have a narrow focus and lack the broad contextual understanding of humans. They often cannot grasp nuanced situations and may make errors if data is incomplete or assumptions are flawed, which is why human oversight is typically needed to supervise automated processes. Augmentation, on the other hand, involves AI assisting human experts and enhancing their capabilities. In

DOI: 10.4324/9781003733881-2

augmentation, humans and AI work together, each contributing unique strengths to accomplish tasks more effectively. For example, in radiology, AI tools can quickly analyze millions of medical scans to flag abnormalities, while human radiologists interpret these results and make decisions using their medical expertise and knowledge of the patient's overall health (Agrawal, Gans, & Goldfarb, 2018). Similarly, in customer service, AI systems can assist human agents by instantly retrieving information or handling simple queries, but human agents provide empathy and personal engagement that AI lacks (Allen & Choudhury, 2022).

To better understand how AI operates, it is useful to view an AI system in terms of three fundamental components: inputs, processes, and outputs. This framework can be further broken down into six building blocks as illustrated in Figure 2.1: structured data, unstructured data, preprocesses, main processes, a knowledge base, and information (Paschen et al., 2020).

The effectiveness of AI in organizations – whether for automation or augmentation – is deeply intertwined with data management. An AI system's performance hinges on the quality, quantity, and accessibility of data. Automation in particular thrives on large amounts of high-quality data to train models, whereas augmentation leverages both data and human insights for informed decision-making. Therefore, organizations must continually evaluate their data resources and anticipate future data needs in alignment with their strategic goals.

AI systems typically deal with two types of inputs: structured and unstructured data. Structured data is highly organized and formatted, making it easy to analyze (for example, sales figures or other numerical business metrics). It often forms the cornerstone of traditional business analytics. Unstructured data, by contrast, includes text, audio, images, and video – formats that lack a predefined structure and are more challenging to analyze. While AI can rapidly process vast quantities of structured data, its ability to extract value from unstructured data

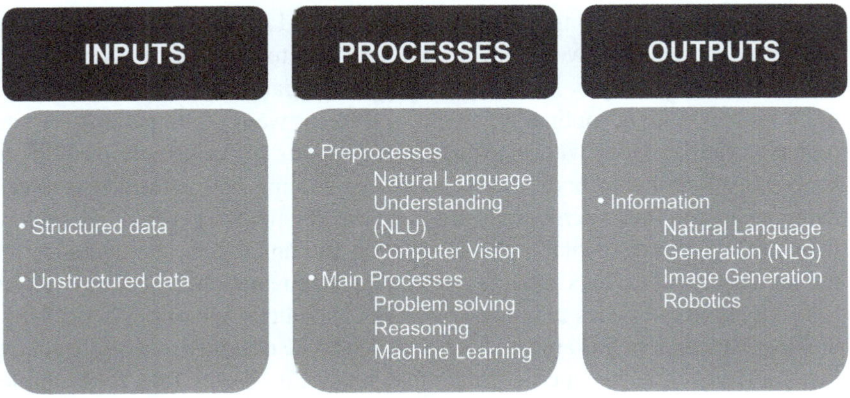

Figure 2.1 Key AI building blocks (adapted from Paschen et al., 2020)

is what truly sets it apart from conventional software. Through natural language processing, AI can interpret human language to identify themes, sentiments, or behaviors in text. AI can also analyze images or videos to recognize objects and interpret visual context.

The operation of AI can be divided into two stages: preprocessing and core processing. In the preprocessing stage, raw data is cleansed and transformed to prepare it for analysis – this step improves data quality and suitability for AI algorithms. The core processing stage is where the "intelligent" work happens: the AI applies problem-solving methods, logical reasoning, and machine learning techniques to the prepared data. These processes often work in concert to achieve the desired outcomes efficiently. For instance, in problem-solving tasks, AI employs divergent thinking to explore many possible solutions and then uses convergent thinking to select the optimal one. Thanks to its ability to handle extremely large datasets, AI excels at this, constantly enriching its knowledge base with new information. AI's reasoning capabilities allow it to infer logical conclusions from available information, even under uncertainty. It can use deductive reasoning (applying general rules to deduce specific conclusions) as well as inductive reasoning (deriving general principles from detailed data). A key aspect of AI's core processing is machine learning, which enables AI systems to act on data and improve over time through experience. Machine learning can be supervised (learning from labeled examples), unsupervised (finding patterns in unlabeled data), or reinforcement learning (learning through trial and error by receiving feedback on success or failure).

The outputs of AI systems are the actionable insights or results produced by these processes. Outputs can take many forms – generating a natural-language report, producing a visual or recommendation, or even controlling a robotic action. These outputs drive a wide range of business applications, from informing strategic decisions with data-driven analyses to automating customer interactions or operational tasks.

With this understanding of inputs, processes, and outputs as a backdrop, we can better appreciate how AI may be applied either to automate tasks or to augment human capabilities in the workplace. The goal in both cases is to integrate AI technologies optimally, albeit in different ways. Automation refers to replacing human labor with machines or algorithms for tasks previously done by people. A growing body of research is examining how effectively AI can automate various tasks across industries and job functions. These studies explore which tasks are most suitable for automation and analyze the implications for productivity, cost savings, and the workforce. Augmentation, by contrast, refers to using AI technologies to enhance human capabilities and improve decision-making. Research in this area looks at how AI can be designed and implemented to complement human expertise rather than replace it – examining, for example, how AI can support collaboration, creativity, or problem-solving in different domains.

For example, studies have shown that AI tools can assist doctors in identifying anomalies in diagnostic images, but the expertise of human radiologists is still needed for accurate interpretation (Choudhury et al., 2020). Similarly, AI can forecast surgical durations with high accuracy, yet it remains important to factor in the judgment of human surgeons in the decision-making process (Ibrahim, Kim, & Tong, 2021). In IT support, AI systems can help address routine service requests, but human experts are required to handle more complex issues (Allen & Choudhury, 2022). Collectively, these examples reinforce that integrating AI is not about the displacement of human expertise but its enhancement. AI's advanced analytical capabilities, combined with the critical thinking and contextual understanding of professionals, create a synergy that can lead to greater efficiency, precision, and innovation. This illustrates how AI's greatest promise lies in partnership with human intelligence, where technology amplifies human skills instead of supplanting them. We should view the evolution of AI in the workplace through this lens: AI as a partner to human ingenuity, providing a scaffold for human intelligence to reach new heights. Rather than rendering professionals obsolete, AI can upskill and empower them to achieve more. This synergistic approach not only boosts productivity but also expands the potential of human talent.

It would be an oversimplification to see AI's impact on work as a strict choice between automation and augmentation. In reality, the most transformative outcomes will likely emerge from combinations of both. For instance, in some areas AI may automate routine, repetitive tasks – freeing human workers to focus on complex, creative, and strategic activities that AI cannot perform. In other cases, AI will primarily augment human work by providing insights from vast datasets that no person could process alone. The strength of automation (efficiency at scale) can complement the strength of human-focused augmentation (contextual judgment and creativity). It is this interplay between automation and augmentation that will define new ways of working, as AI and humans co-create value in ways neither could achieve independently.

The studies mentioned above – from medical diagnostics to IT support – illustrate that AI's role is to bolster human capability, not replace it. The emerging reality is that AI will not simply take over tasks; it will also provide a platform on which human intelligence can climb to new heights. By embracing AI as a collaborator, professionals are more likely to be upskilled and empowered rather than made obsolete. In practical terms, an AI tool often serves as an assistant that elevates the quality and efficiency of human work. Through this lens, AI in the workplace becomes a partner to human ingenuity, not its adversary. This partnership promises not just higher productivity, but an expansion of human potential.

Building on this understanding, Holmström and Carroll (2025) identify four generic innovation strategies based on two key dimensions: automation and augmentation (each of which can be either high or low). As outlined in Figure 2.2, the four strategies are: "Traditional Tool" (low automation, low augmentation), "Basic Automation" (high automation, low augmentation), "Automated

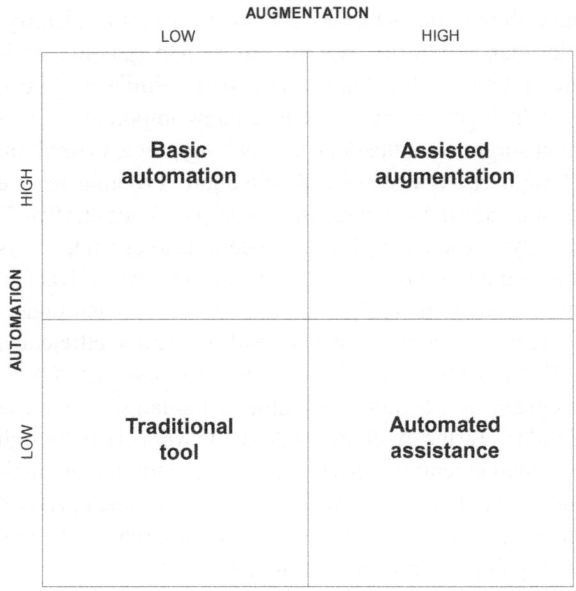

Figure 2.2 Strategies for innovating with AI (Holmström & Carroll, 2025)

Assistance" (low automation, high augmentation), and "Assisted Augmentation" (high automation, high augmentation). Each strategy has distinct characteristics and comes with different risks, challenges, and management tactics.

Traditional tool: This approach to innovation involves low levels of both automation and augmentation. It relies heavily on human expertise, with technology playing only a minor, supporting role. Traditional tools lack the advanced AI-driven capabilities of modern approaches, but they still have value in that they leverage human creativity and knowledge. Such tools maintain basic operations and foster innovation through human effort, without significant help from automation or intelligent augmentation.

Basic automation: This strategy features high automation and low augmentation. AI technologies here are used primarily to streamline processes and increase efficiency, rather than to contribute creatively. In a basic automation approach, AI optimizes and accelerates existing workflows by taking over routine, repetitive tasks. While this can greatly improve productivity and reduce costs, it typically does not enhance the organization's creative problem-solving or generate novel innovations – its impact on innovation is mostly indirect, via efficiency gains.

Automated assistance: In this scenario, technology is used to augment human skills and creativity within the innovation process. It combines human ingenuity with advanced AI tools to enhance problem-solving and idea generation. AI acts as an assistant that provides data-driven insights, reduces manual effort, and improves the efficiency of developing new ideas. For example, an AI system might analyze large datasets to suggest product improvements or market opportunities, which human team members can then evaluate and build upon. This approach keeps human creativity at the forefront, with AI as a supportive force.

Assisted augmentation: This strategy represents the highest levels of both automation and augmentation. Advanced technologies play a central role in driving innovation, automating many aspects of the process while also significantly enhancing human creative capabilities. In an assisted augmentation model, AI might handle complex analyses and routine decisions at scale, enabling human innovators to focus on high-level creativity and strategy. The result is a powerful combination: businesses can streamline their innovation processes and simultaneously explore more ambitious, innovative solutions. This approach is well-suited to fast-changing environments where companies must rapidly adapt and innovate to stay competitive.

Using this framework, organizations can align their innovation objectives with the appropriate AI strategy – whether the goal is to enhance creative processes or to improve operational efficiency. In practice, the best performance often comes from a balanced combination of human and AI strengths, rather than relying on either one alone. As suggested by Figure 2.2, an organization typically achieves superior results when it melds human expertise with AI capabilities. Furthermore, as AI technologies continue to evolve, the line between what is automation and what is augmentation may increasingly blur. Organizations will need to remain flexible, integrating AI in ways that leverage both its automating power and its ability to augment human talent.

The research agenda on AI-supported work performance is rapidly expanding and covers a broad range of topics. These include the development of new AI technologies, the dynamics of human-AI interaction, organizational factors that influence AI adoption, and the ethical considerations of AI in the workplace. By examining outcomes of both automation and augmentation, researchers aim to build a comprehensive understanding of AI's role in the future of work. The insights from this research will be critical for guiding organizations as they strive to harness AI's potential while also addressing the technical and human challenges that accompany its implementation.

Data work

The notion of "data work" has become increasingly important as AI becomes more and more used in organizations. Data work encompasses all the tasks and processes involved in creating, managing, and interpreting data. In AI development, data work is especially crucial: beyond simply collecting and cleaning data, it extends to analyzing and interpreting data in order to train and refine AI models. For example, in healthcare, data work is integral to patient care and medical research (e.g. compiling patient records, lab results, and medical images to improve diagnoses and treatments). In education, data about student performance and engagement is analyzed to inform teaching methods and curriculum design. Clearly, data work does not come without challenges: organizations must ensure data quality, manage large volumes of information, and address privacy and security concerns. Despite these difficulties, however, effective data work offers significant benefits. It can lead to better-performing AI systems, more informed and objective decision-making, and even the creation of new jobs and skill sets in the data and AI fields.

To fully grasp the essence of data work, it is helpful to clarify what we mean by data in an organizational context. The role of data in innovation can actually be understood in three distinct ways. Below are three perspectives on how data contributes to innovation, each illustrating a different concept of "data-driven" work:

Data-driven innovation: In this mode, organizations use data analytics and AI as tools to improve existing products, services, or strategies. Here, data is a catalyst for new insights that inform decision-making. For example, a company might analyze customer data to discover new market segments and then tailor products to those segments. A well-known example is Netflix using viewers' streaming data to decide which new series to produce and how to personalize recommendations for its users. Here, data itself isn't the end product – it is a means to enhance the effectiveness of strategies and offerings.

Data-based innovation: This refers to innovations that are fundamentally built out of data. In these cases, the product or service is the data, or it would not exist without the underlying data making it possible. Credit scores, for instance, are an innovation entirely constituted by data – they aggregate financial data into a score that affects lending decisions. Popularity metrics (like social media follower counts or trending topics) are another example of a creation that is purely data-based. Unlike data-driven innovation, which uses data to improve something external, data-based innovation means the value is embedded in the data itself.

Data creation as innovation: Sometimes the act of producing new data, or new forms of data, is an innovation in its own right. This involves developing novel methods of capturing and representing phenomena as data, often enabling analysis of things that were not quantifiable before. One example is the creation of standardized GPS data formats. By translating raw satellite signals into a universal digital format for location, GPS data unlocked innovations from real-time navigation systems to geospatial analysis. This type of innovation is about turning complex, previously unstructured aspects of the world into structured data that can be computed and analyzed.

Recognizing these distinctions is crucial because each perspective on data calls for different approaches and skills in data work. Analyzing patterns in existing data to inform decisions (data-driven innovation) is a different kind of work than quantifying an intangible concept into data (data-based innovation), or designing a new data format to capture an entirely new phenomenon (data creation as innovation). Understanding what kind of data role is at play in a given project allows organizations to take a more nuanced approach, applying the right methodologies and expertise to get the most value from their data.

The impact of data work extends beyond individual tasks or roles – it is reshaping entire job functions and even giving rise to new professions devoted to data management and analysis. Organizations are adapting too, often undergoing structural changes to accommodate the growing importance of data work. In an AI-driven organization, data work is central to leveraging the value of AI because it provides the foundation on which AI models are built, trained, and improved. A successful AI deployment depends on having high-quality data that is well-prepared, diverse, and truly representative of the domain in which the AI operates. To maximize the value of AI, it is essential to create a collaborative data work environment that brings together AI specialists and domain experts effectively.

Data work is not a static, one-time effort – it is dynamic and often bidirectional. This means data work requires understanding how data has been collected and used historically and how it might be used in the future. It frequently involves cross-disciplinary expertise and is influenced by the knowledge frameworks (or "epistemologies") of specific industries. For instance, consider the oil and gas industry: subsurface geological data represents a physical reality that is difficult to access, and making that data useful requires a deep understanding of geology and engineering. A longitudinal case study of data work in Norway's oil and gas sector described it as a complex set of practices requiring continuous context-building around the data (Parmiggiani et al., 2022). In that context, data workers had to engage in data discovery ("getting the right data") and data preparation ("getting the data right") in a dynamic socio-technical environment – constantly framing and reframing data to address evolving questions and challenges.

More often than not, data work is highly collaborative. People from various disciplines must work together to find, manage, and interpret data. A significant amount of "backroom" effort goes into activities like locating the appropriate data sources, cleaning and standardizing data, and managing it securely. Only after this preparation can the "front-stage" work of analysis and insight-generation occur. Importantly, this behind-the-scenes labor is qualitatively different from the visible analytics or AI modeling, yet it is deeply intertwined with those outcomes. In other words, without extensive groundwork in data curation and preparation, the advanced analytics would neither be possible nor trustworthy.

Within an organization, effective data work often depends on close collaboration between two groups: AI experts and domain experts. AI experts contribute a deep understanding of algorithms, data processing techniques, and how to fine-tune models for optimal performance. They know how to craft and improve AI systems to meet technical requirements. Domain experts, on the other hand, bring in-depth knowledge of the field in which the AI is applied – be it healthcare, finance, education, or any other domain. They understand the context, the nuances, and the practical challenges in that field. This contextual intelligence is vital to ensure that AI solutions are relevant, useful, and address the real needs of the domain.

When AI specialists and domain specialists form a partnership, their combined expertise bridges the gap between advanced technology and real-world application. In a collaborative data work setting, each side plays a distinct but complementary role. Domain experts help identify which data is relevant, provide context to interpret that data correctly, and highlight the key factors that an AI model should consider for the solution to be meaningful. AI experts then apply their technical skills to process, clean, and transform the data, and they develop and optimize the AI models based on that data. This kind of cross-functional teamwork ensures that the resulting AI system is both technically sound and contextually appropriate.

Deliberate boundary-spanning efforts can further strengthen collaboration between AI experts and domain experts. This involves creating opportunities for regular communication and knowledge sharing – such as joint meetings, workshops, or integrated project teams – so that each group gains a better understanding of the other's perspectives, requirements, and constraints. Such interactions help surface potential issues early, whether it is a concern about data quality, awareness of a bias in the dataset, or a misalignment between what the AI outputs and what the domain really needs. By actively bridging these gaps, an organization can ensure its AI systems are not built in isolation by technologists, but rather co-designed with input from those who understand the domain. This alignment makes AI solutions more relevant and increases the likelihood of user acceptance and successful implementation.

Many tasks related to data in organizations are sometimes perceived as mundane prerequisites – chores that must be done before the "real work" of building models or algorithms can begin. However, it is crucial to recognize that data quality is a foundation for everything that follows. Ensuring high data quality is as important to AI success as debugging is to software development. Just as engineers rigorously test software for bugs before deploying it, data scientists and managers need to test for defects or issues in data with equal rigor. Poor-quality data can introduce weaknesses into machine learning models that may not be apparent until after deployment. As organizations lean more on data-driven AI tools to make decisions, having high-quality data becomes absolutely critical – without it, these tools cannot learn effectively or improve their performance over time. For example, training an AI system to diagnose medical conditions might require thousands of labeled medical images. Obtaining this volume of quality data is not as simple as pulling automatically generated "digital exhaust" from day-to-day operations; it often requires dedicated effort to gather and curate the right data (Lebovitz et al., 2021).

Recent research highlights that obtaining and maintaining data is itself a complex form of work. It involves activities like searching for the right datasets, sharing data across silos, and ongoing maintenance of data resources (Aaltonen et al., 2021). As the demand for data increases within organizations, employees might be pressured to change how they do their jobs in order to produce data that is more easily analyzable by algorithms. New data entry procedures, documentation requirements, or process changes might be introduced so that operations generate cleaner or more structured data. These shifts can lead to conflicts and resistance from employees who feel that the new requirements disrupt their established routines or professional autonomy. The implications of such resistance are multifaceted: it can slow down the adoption of AI tools, and it can also affect morale and the culture of the workplace. This is a strong reminder that integrating AI into organizational processes is as much a human and managerial challenge as it is a technical one.

Building a data-driven environment thus demands more than just technology – it requires a transformation in organizational culture. Leaders and managers need to foster an atmosphere that embraces change, encourages adaptability, and supports continuous learning. Employees should understand why new data practices are important and how they contribute to larger goals. Overcoming resistance often involves a delicate balance: providing incentives and support for employees to adopt new practices, aligning those practices with the organization's existing values and mission, and clearly communicating the benefits of the changes. Managers may need to champion data initiatives and address concerns empathetically, showing employees that their knowledge and experience are still valued in an AI-enabled workplace. Ultimately, the successful integration of AI tools depends on this negotiation between technological imperatives and human factors.

From a managerial perspective, it is important to recognize that acquiring the data needed for AI tools is rarely a straightforward task. Managers should anticipate that new data requirements might necessitate changes in how employees work, and they should be prepared to manage the frictions that arise from such changes. In fact, understanding the tensions associated with obtaining data for

AI is so critical that the authors of this work propose a theoretical framework to conceptualize them. This framework focuses on the divergent interests and viewpoints of two key groups in the data workflow: the data scientists (or AI developers) who need ample, high-quality data for modeling, and the front-line users or professionals who generate and use data as part of their jobs. Often, data scientists demand data in a form that is convenient for algorithms, while practitioners care about data that fits their practical needs – which can lead to tension. By taking a boundary-spanning lens, the framework will examine how these differences are negotiated through emerging practices within organizations. The goal is to help managers navigate conflicts by highlighting where interests diverge and how collaboration and communication can bridge those gaps.

In summary, data work is a multifaceted and evolving set of tasks that plays a critical role in any effort to create value from AI. It presents both challenges and opportunities across virtually all sectors. As technology continues to advance, recognizing the value of data work – and investing in it – will be essential for future innovation and progress. Above all, data work is the foundation for leveraging AI effectively in any organization. Integrating the efforts of AI experts and domain experts in a collaborative setting is key to maximizing AI's potential. Strong boundary-spanning practices facilitate communication and mutual understanding between technical and business stakeholders, ensuring that AI systems are both robust and relevant. This collaboration drives value creation and can provide a competitive advantage. It is also important to note that measuring data quality remains a nebulous task; "ground truth" data (against which models are tested) can itself be imperfect or biased. Common challenges include biases in labeled datasets, errors or inconsistencies in data, limitations of standard benchmarks, difficulties in reproducing results, and a lack of proper data documentation. Managers must be aware of these data quality issues and work proactively to address them. Since data is such a crucial asset for AI, its quality and integrity should be managed with rigorous standards to ensure that AI models accurately represent and predict real-world phenomena. In short, treating data with the same care as any mission-critical resource is essential for any organization looking to succeed with AI.

The old adage "data is the new oil" captures the essence of the digital economy, underscoring that data has become a key driver of value today. Just as oil fueled the industrial revolution, data fuels innovation and economic growth in the digital revolution. Organizations that leverage AI are tapping into this resource, with data serving as the cornerstone for developing sophisticated AI models. Those models, through complex algorithms, sift through vast amounts of raw data and refine it into actionable insights – much like refining crude oil into gasoline and other useful products. The parallel with oil extends to the effort required: just as oil must be extracted, processed, and refined, data must be collected, cleaned, and analyzed to be truly useful. Data refinement involves ensuring quality, removing noise and errors, and structuring the information in a way that AI systems can interpret. The insights gained from this refined data can be incredibly valuable, informing everything from understanding consumer behavior and predicting market trends to enhancing operational efficiency and personalizing user experiences.

However, it is also important to recognize the differences between data and oil. Oil is a finite resource and often a source of geopolitical conflict; data, by contrast, is effectively renewable and is generated continuously by digital activities. Every online interaction, sensor reading, or transaction creates new data. This means data can be an ever-refreshing wellspring for AI systems, allowing them to learn and improve continuously. The more high-quality data an AI system can consume, the more it can refine its capabilities, giving organizations a growing opportunity to innovate and create value over time. This abundance of data, combined with powerful AI capabilities, creates a synergy that can unlock transformative potential across industries. For example, in healthcare, aggregating and analyzing patient data can lead to breakthroughs in personalized medicine. In urban planning, traffic and mobility data can be used to optimize city layouts and reduce congestion. The possible applications of data-fueled AI are boundless.

Yet with great potential comes great responsibility. Organizations must address issues of privacy, security, and ethical use of data – the "new oil" must be handled in a way that ensures the future it powers is not only prosperous but also fair and respectful of individual rights. This necessity brings the concept of data governance to the forefront. Companies need to navigate complex questions about data ownership, consent, and compliance with regulations, balancing the pursuit of innovation with the imperative of maintaining public trust. As AI systems become more deeply embedded in society's fabric, managing data responsibly will become as critical as environmental stewardship has been in the age of oil. In conclusion, while data shares some characteristics with oil in its capacity to generate value, its unique properties and the context of its use in AI demand a nuanced understanding. Organizations must approach data with strategies that recognize its renewable nature, its ethical implications, and its broader impact on society.

As data is becoming more and more valuable as currency, the role of data work becomes increasingly strategic. To reap the full potential of data, data workers and managers should focus on a few key initiatives that help extract value from this asset. This encompasses several efforts:

Develop a data governance framework: Establish clear rules and processes for how data is collected, stored, and used. Good data governance builds trust in data by defining who is responsible for it and how quality is maintained.

Invest in data infrastructure: Provide the necessary technology and tools to store, process, and analyze large amounts of data. This may involve cloud storage solutions, data warehousing, analytics and visualization platforms, and machine learning infrastructure. A strong data infrastructure ensures that data can flow efficiently through the organization and be readily accessible for AI and analytics tasks.

Build data competencies: Develop the skills and expertise needed to work effectively with data and AI. This includes training employees in data science, machine learning, and big data technologies, as well as in data interpretation and critical thinking. Hiring or upskilling talent in these areas will ensure the organization has the human capabilities to extract insights from data.

Foster a culture of data-driven decision-making: Cultivate an organizational culture where data is routinely used to inform decisions at all levels. Leaders should encourage employees to support proposals and evaluate outcomes with data where possible. This might involve providing staff with access to relevant data and analytical tools, and rewarding evidence-based decision processes. The goal is to make using data a natural part of how the organization operates.

Leverage data for innovation: Encourage creative thinking about how data can lead to new products, services, or business models. This could mean experimenting with emerging technologies like natural language processing, computer vision, or reinforcement learning to find novel ways to analyze data. It could also involve looking at how data partnerships or open data could create opportunities. Organizations that approach data with an innovative mindset can discover new revenue streams or efficiencies that weren't evident before.

While data is indeed a critical asset for organizations, its true value is unlocked not by sheer volume but through deliberate and strategic effort. In this light, managers play a central role in cultivating an ecosystem where data is translated into value. To capitalize on data, organizations should first put in place robust data governance frameworks. Such frameworks not only ensure the quality and integrity of data, but also address legal and ethical considerations. Investing in data infrastructure is equally vital: scalable and secure systems form the backbone for data work. They enable the efficient storage, processing, and analysis of large datasets. Developing data competencies across the workforce is another strategic priority. This involves training employees in data literacy and analytics so they have the skills to interpret data and derive insights in their roles. Beyond individual skills, creating a culture of data-driven decision-making is crucial – when decisions at all levels are informed by data, they tend to be more objective and effective. Finally, leveraging data for innovation is key to gaining a competitive edge. Data can reveal patterns and opportunities that drive product development, optimize customer experiences, or even point to entirely new business models. By embracing a data-centric approach to innovation, organizations can pioneer new solutions and adapt to market changes. In sum, the path to creating value from data and AI is multifaceted. It requires alignment between data initiatives and business strategy, a supportive culture, and continuous investment in both technology and talent. Organizations that treat data as a strategic asset – integrating it into their core operations – are better positioned to innovate, outperform competitors, and lead in their industries.

How to create value from data and AI: The five habits of highly effective AI organizations

AI technologies have dramatically changed how we think about and utilize data. Before AI became mainstream, data was expensive to acquire, challenging to store, and often confined to departmental silos within an organization. Now, data is being generated at an extraordinary pace by virtually every online action, every sensor output, and the digitization of everyday activities. This shift has been monumental: data has transformed from a static, underused asset into a dynamic, continuous flow that organizations can tap into. Not only do companies produce data; individuals contribute vast amounts with each digital interaction. For managers and decision-makers, it is critical to realize that an AI system's effectiveness is inherently tied to the quality of the data it learns from. The phrase "garbage in, garbage out" succinctly captures this point: if an AI is trained on flawed or low-quality data, it will produce flawed outputs, potentially compounding errors or biases on a large scale. This underscores the central importance of data quality management in any AI initiative.

The risk of relying on faulty data in AI highlights the need for strong data governance. Managers must establish protocols and standards for data acquisition, cleansing, processing, and analysis to minimize the introduction of biases or inaccuracies into AI models. It is not merely about collecting large volumes of data, but about curating high-fidelity datasets that enable AI systems to perform with precision and reliability. In many cases, data's true value is also underappreciated because organizations do not fully consider its compounding benefit over time. Data collected today can provide immediate insights and also become part of a larger historical dataset that yields deep, longitudinal understanding of trends. Moreover, the rapid expansion of data generation presents both challenges and opportunities: with the right analytic tools, this data can be harnessed to personalize customer experiences, streamline operations, and inspire new business models that were not previously possible. Navigating this landscape requires managers to recognize data's strategic value and invest appropriately in infrastructure and talent. As such, data should be treated as a core strategic asset. By investing in data quality and governance, organizations set the stage to unlock AI's full potential. Only with clean, well-governed data can AI reliably drive innovation, efficiency, and growth.

In recent years, the convergence of vastly increased data availability, greater computing power, and improved algorithms has enabled AI applications that were once thought impossible (Ransbotham et al., 2017). AI's rapid advancement has drawn significant attention from researchers and practitioners, who are exploring the technology's potential value to organizations and investigating how it can enhance tasks that traditionally required human judgment and manual effort (Berente et al., 2021). A key factor in AI's leap forward has been progress in deep learning – multi-layered neural network models capable of self-learning and making highly accurate predictions. These advances have significantly expanded AI's capabilities beyond the limitations of earlier-generation AI tools (Lecun et al., 2015). As a result, AI has emerged as a transformative force across industries, fueling innovation and providing a distinct competitive edge to those who wield it effectively. Its ability to synthesize and analyze vast amounts of data in real time makes it invaluable for enhancing decision-making and operational efficiency. Consider a few examples: In human resources, AI is used to streamline recruitment by scanning candidate profiles and identifying those that best match job requirements. In customer service, AI-driven virtual assistants handle routine inquiries through natural language conversations, providing timely and contextually relevant responses to users. Indeed, AI has become a staple in the modern professional landscape, particularly in domains where digital technology and data analytics are central. Its applications are vast and varied – ranging from predictive analytics in finance that detect fraud or inform investment decisions, to personalized learning platforms in education that adapt to each student's needs. Crucially, AI is not only about automating tasks; it is equally about augmenting human capabilities and allowing us to tackle complex problems with greater precision and insight.

Despite the well-recognized potential of AI, recent studies suggest that implementing AI in organizations and actually capturing value from it remains challenging (Sundberg & Holmström, 2023). Successfully deploying AI often requires changes across many parts of an organization – technology infrastructure, workflows, employee skills, and even organizational boundaries and goals. An important aspect in meeting this challenge is what Holmström (2022) calls AI readiness, defined as "the ability to deploy AI technologies to enable digital transformation, in four key dimensions: technologies, activities, boundaries, and goals." In essence, AI readiness is a measure of how prepared an organization is to integrate AI into its operations and strategy. In the discussion that follows, we focus on organizational habits that can enhance AI readiness. AI's capability to process large volumes of data, discern patterns, and improve outcomes offers significant value, but to fully harness these benefits, organizations must cultivate certain habits and routines that foster the effective use of AI.

Building on studies of habits as fundamental to taking action (Farjoun & Mahmood, 2023) and on the emerging field of AI management (Berente et al., 2021), we propose five key habits that underlie successful engagements with AI in organizations. Emphasizing these habits underscores the importance of deliberate design and planning in using AI. The idea is that by developing good organizational habits and routines, companies can ensure that AI systems align with their goals and values, leading to greater success and impact. We will explore each of these five habits in detail:

Get the data right: Data is the backbone of today's AI systems, so ensuring data quality and integrity ("getting the data right") is a crucial first habit. AI systems learn and make predictions based on the data they are given; if that data is flawed or irrelevant, the AI's outputs will be unreliable – a clear case of "garbage in, garbage out." Therefore, organizations must prioritize data integrity to guarantee meaningful AI-driven insights. Maintaining high data quality is a complex undertaking involving multiple dimensions:

Data collection: Here, it is important for organizations to gather relevant, high-quality data that truly represents the real-world scenarios where the AI will operate. It is important to ensure the dataset is diverse and comprehensive enough to cover the variations the AI might encounter.
Data cleaning: Organizations need to remove and/or correct erroneous, incomplete, or irrelevant data. This step addresses issues like duplicate records, inconsistencies, or inaccuracies that could skew AI processing.
Data updating: Organizations must keep data up to date. Regularly updating datasets ensures that AI systems have the latest data – especially critical in dynamic environments (for example, using recent sales data in a forecasting model).
Data management: It is imperative for organizations to organize and store data in ways that make it accessible and usable for those who need it. As such, good data management involves structuring data (through databases or data warehouses), securing it, and handling it ethically – particularly when it comes to personal or sensitive information.
Data quality assurance: Organizations must implement ongoing checks and monitoring to detect any corruption, degradation, or anomalies in the data.
Data governance: Organizations must establish clear policies and frameworks for how data is handled throughout its life cycle. Data governance covers who can access data, how privacy is protected, how long data is kept, and how compliance with laws and regulations is maintained. A strong governance framework helps maintain high standards for data and builds trust in its use.

Investment in data infrastructure: Organizations need to be willing to invest in tools and systems that can handle data effectively. This includes scalable storage solutions, processing power for big data analytics, and platforms for managing data pipelines. Without adequate infrastructure, even well-collected data cannot be fully utilized.

Training and awareness: Organizations must educate employees about the importance of data quality and their role in maintaining it. Everyone who handles data should know how to do so properly and understand the impact of their actions on data integrity. Building a data-aware culture means that individuals take responsibility for the quality of the data they touch.

By focusing on these areas, organizations can improve the reliability of their AI systems. High-quality data leads to more accurate predictions, smarter insights, and better decision-making. Moreover, as AI continues to evolve, the demand for quality data will only increase – making this habit of "getting the data right" an indispensable foundation for any AI-driven initiative.

Build the necessary AI skills: Equipping the organization with the necessary AI-related skills is essential to harness the full potential of AI technologies. As AI tools and techniques evolve at breakneck speed, companies must ensure their workforce keeps pace – not only in technical prowess but also in understanding the broader implications of AI, such as ethical considerations and bias mitigation. Building AI skills involves multiple facets:

Technical proficiency: Provide comprehensive training in the core technical domains of AI – data science, machine learning, statistics, and the programming languages or frameworks commonly used for AI development. This can be achieved through in-house training programs, online courses, workshops, or partnerships with educational institutions. The goal is to develop a cadre of employees who can develop, interpret, and maintain AI systems.

Continual learning: Recognize that learning about AI is not a one-time event. The field is evolving rapidly, so create mechanisms for continuous education. Encourage employees to update their skills and stay current with new AI techniques and tools.

Ethics and bias awareness: Train staff to identify and mitigate biases in AI algorithms and datasets. Include instruction on the ethical implications of AI – such as fairness, accountability, and transparency – so that teams consider these factors when developing or deploying AI solutions. An ethically aware team is more likely to catch issues like biased training data or unintended consequences of an AI model before they become bigger problems.

Collaboration and communication: Because AI projects often span multiple departments, employees should learn to work in interdisciplinary teams and communicate technical concepts to non-technical stakeholders (and vice versa). Strong communication and collaboration skills ensure that AI initiatives have the support and understanding of the whole organization and that technical teams understand the real-world problems they are trying to solve.

Regulatory knowledge: As AI adoption grows, so does scrutiny from regulators. Teams should stay informed about relevant laws, standards, and compliance requirements related to data protection, AI usage, and industry-specific regulations.

Creating an AI-friendly culture: Beyond individual skills, it is important to foster a culture that is receptive to innovation and comfortable with change. Encourage experimentation with AI, accept that some initiatives may fail and treat them as learning opportunities, and cultivate a mindset that looks to leverage AI for solving problems. Leadership should visibly support AI projects and celebrate data-driven successes to reinforce this culture.

By investing in these areas, organizations ensure that their teams are not only prepared for the AI of today but are also adaptable for the AI of tomorrow. Having a skilled and knowledgeable workforce provides a sustainable competitive edge in an AI-driven world, as it enables a company to innovate rapidly and use AI responsibly and effectively.

Create diverse and multidisciplinary AI teams: AI projects benefit immensely from diversity of thought and expertise. Therefore, organizations should form multidisciplinary teams for AI initiatives, bringing together people with a variety of skills and backgrounds – data scientists, AI engineers, business analysts, domain specialists, and even experts in ethics or social science. Diversity here doesn't only refer to job role or technical skill; it also encompasses different cognitive perspectives, cultural backgrounds, and life experiences. Such diversity can greatly enhance a team's problem-solving abilities. There are several reasons why diverse, multidisciplinary teams are so valuable for AI projects:

Broader problem-solving approaches: Team members from different disciplines will approach a problem from different angles. For example, a data scientist might focus on the numerical patterns in customer data, while a psychologist on the team might consider human behavioral factors influencing those patterns. This mix of approaches can lead to more creative and effective solutions because the team examines challenges from multiple viewpoints.

Mitigating biases: AI systems are prone to biases, especially if the development team is homogeneous or if the data reflects only a narrow slice of reality. A diverse team is more likely to spot blind spots and question assumptions that others take for granted. By including people of different genders, cultures, and backgrounds, the team can better identify potential biases in the data or in the model's behavior and work to correct them, leading to better AI outcomes.

Enhanced communication and outreach: A team that includes members with varied expertise is often better at communicating the benefits, risks, and workings of an AI system to a broad audience. They can translate technical jargon into business implications or societal impact. This is crucial when it comes to getting buy-in from stakeholders who may not be technically versed, such as executives, customers, or regulatory bodies.

Innovation and competitiveness: Different perspectives can spark innovation. When team members challenge each other's ideas and introduce new concepts from their fields, it can lead to breakthrough applications of AI. This creative synergy can give an organization a competitive edge as it is more likely to develop unique solutions that competitors (perhaps working in silos) might not arrive at.

Resilience and adaptability: Teams that are diverse in skills and thinking styles tend to be more resilient. If unforeseen challenges arise during AI development (and they often do), a multidisciplinary team can adapt by leveraging its wide range of expertise. They are better equipped to handle new kinds of problems, whether technical glitches, user experience issues, or ethical dilemmas, because someone on the team is likely to have relevant knowledge or a novel way of looking at the issue.

For these reasons, it is crucial for organizations not only to hire individuals with varied skills, but also to foster an inclusive environment where different ideas and perspectives are valued. This means encouraging open dialogue, ensuring all team members have a voice, and creating a culture of respect and curiosity. The outcome is AI systems that are not only technologically advanced, but also more socially aware, user-friendly, and robust against a variety of real-world scenarios.

Establish an ecosystem strategy for AI: No organization operates in isolation, especially when it comes to technology. Establishing an ecosystem strategy for AI means understanding how AI fits into the bigger picture of the organization's goals and its external environment. In practice, this habit involves aligning AI initiatives with the overall business strategy, considering how AI interacts with other technologies and processes, and determining how external partnerships and collaborations can enhance AI efforts. Key dimensions to consider include:

Alignment with organizational objectives: Every AI project should support a clear business goal or solve a meaningful problem. Whether the objective is to improve customer service, increase operational efficiency, or drive innovation in product development, the AI strategy must tie back to these overarching goals. This alignment ensures AI investments deliver tangible value and are recognized as strategic, not just experimental tech endeavors.

Interoperability with existing systems: Most companies have significant existing IT systems and processes. An effective AI ecosystem strategy accounts for how new AI tools will integrate with legacy systems and workflows. This might involve upgrading IT infrastructure, using APIs to connect AI services with current software, or choosing AI platforms that are compatible with the company's data formats and IT standards. Smooth interoperability prevents the AI initiative from becoming a silo and helps it scale across the organization.

Data strategy integration: Since AI is heavily dependent on data, the AI strategy must be entwined with the organization's data strategy. Considerations include how data is collected (and from where), how it is governed and kept secure, and how data flows within the organization. A well-integrated data strategy ensures that AI teams have access to the data they need and that data-related issues (quality, privacy, etc.) are managed in harmony with AI development.

Cultural integration: Successful AI adoption often requires a cultural shift. Stakeholders at all levels should understand the value that AI brings and be willing to adapt to changes in their workflows. This could involve training programs, internal evangelism of AI success stories, and engaging employees in pilot projects so they feel a sense of ownership.

Talent and knowledge development: Part of an AI ecosystem approach is ensuring you have the right people in place. This might mean hiring new talent, but it also includes upskilling current employees. An organization might develop an internal "AI academy" or encourage cross-training so that there's a broad base of AI knowledge.

Participating in the wider innovation ecosystem: Beyond the organization's walls, there's a whole ecosystem of AI innovation – startups, universities, research institutions, and industry consortia. Engaging with this ecosystem can provide early access to new developments, foster collaborations (for example, partnerships with startups or research labs), and help in recruiting talent. It may also involve contributing to open source projects or industry standards. By participating in the broader AI community, an organization stays at the cutting edge and can often do more than it could alone.

Scalability and future-proofing: An ecosystem perspective also means planning for the future. As AI solutions prove their value, the organization should be ready to scale them up. This involves anticipating the computational resources and data storage needed for larger deployments, as well as thinking about maintainability and flexibility of AI systems so they can evolve with the business's needs.

By considering these dimensions, organizations can develop an AI ecosystem strategy that ensures technology is not implemented as a mere afterthought or isolated tool, but rather is woven into the fabric of the company's strategy and operations. This holistic approach leads to more sustainable success and a stronger competitive position in the AI space.

Use AI to facilitate organizational learning: The fifth habit is to actively use AI as a tool for organizational learning. AI has tremendous potential to help organizations learn and improve by capturing knowledge, revealing insights, and speeding up feedback cycles. Cultivating a habit of using AI in this way can lead to smarter decision-making, better processes, and a more adaptive, successful organization overall. AI systems can process and analyze information at a scale and speed far beyond human capabilities, turning raw data into actionable knowledge. However, it is important to emphasize that AI should supplement human decision-making, not completely replace the human element. Some ways AI can foster a learning organization include:

Knowledge management: AI can help organize and retrieve the vast amounts of knowledge that accumulate in an organization. For example, natural language processing can be used to index and search through documents, emails, and reports, making it easier for employees to find relevant information and past learnings. AI can also detect patterns in how knowledge is used and suggest ways to fill gaps or connect people with similar knowledge needs.

Insight generation: Through techniques like data mining and predictive analytics, AI can uncover new insights about markets, customer behavior, and internal operations. These insights might not be obvious and could be missed by humans poring over raw data. By highlighting trends (like an emerging customer preference or an inefficiency in a supply chain), AI provides learning opportunities that can drive innovation and strategic adjustments.

Continuous improvement: AI can monitor the outcomes of business processes in real time and learn from them. For instance, an AI system could analyze production line data to detect when output starts to drift from the norm, or it could observe customer interactions to suggest improvements in service processes. By continuously evaluating performance and outcomes, AI enables a feedback loop where processes are incrementally adjusted and improved based on data-driven evidence.

Personalized learning for employees: AI can also facilitate the learning and development of an organization's employees. Adaptive learning systems can customize training content to an employee's needs, pace, and learning style, which helps individuals upskill more effectively. Over time, an AI-powered learning platform can help the workforce acquire new skills that the organization needs in a flexible and scalable way.

Decision support: AI can act as a powerful decision-support tool by providing data-driven recommendations or highlighting key factors to consider. This can help reduce human biases in decision-making and ensure that decisions are based on evidence. For example, an AI system might flag anomalous transactions for a finance team to review, or suggest optimal inventory levels for a retail business by forecasting demand. Humans remain in the loop to apply judgment and consider context, but AI ensures they're equipped with the best possible information.

Automated analysis of experiments: If an organization is regularly trying new things (new product features, marketing campaigns, process tweaks), AI can automate the analysis of these experiments. It can quickly identify what worked and what did not work, controlling for various factors, and thus help the organization learn from both successes and failures more efficiently.

Collaboration enhancement: AI tools can also improve how teams collaborate. For example, AI might analyze communication patterns (while respecting privacy) to recommend more effective team structures or to identify expertise within the company. It could also provide platforms where insights from different departments are shared and synthesized, showing how one team's learnings might apply in another context. By demonstrating the value of data and insights in everyday work, AI encourages a culture that values evidence-based, collaborative learning.

Scalable learning: One of AI's advantages is that it can handle increasing volumes of data without needing breaks or more manpower. As the organization grows, AI systems can scale the learning process – digesting more information and continuing to provide timely analysis – without a proportional increase in time or cost. This allows large organizations to remain agile and informed similarly to a small startup that learns and pivots quickly.

Organizations that leverage AI effectively for learning will not only improve their operations but also gain a competitive advantage by being more adaptable and responsive to change. The key is to maintain a balance where AI supports and amplifies human intelligence rather than attempting to replace it. Human judgment, curiosity, and creativity remain essential, especially when it comes to interpreting insights and making strategic decisions. AI provides the tools to learn faster and more deeply, but humans provide the wisdom on how to act on that learning.

By fostering these five habits, organizations can optimize the integration and utilization of AI, aligning it with their goals and values for improved outcomes. It begins with the foundational step of ensuring data accuracy and integrity, since quality data is the cornerstone of effective AI. Organizations must put in place strong data management processes so that the data feeding their AI algorithms is reliable and representative. Additionally, building AI literacy and technical skills across the organization is essential. This means not only training those who develop AI, but also educating decision-makers and employees who will work alongside AI, so that they understand what AI can and cannot do. Investing in education and skill development empowers teams to leverage AI innovatively and responsibly.

The creation of diverse and multidisciplinary teams is another critical habit. Such teams bring together varied perspectives and expertise, creating an environment where creative solutions to complex problems can flourish. Diversity in thought and background also helps mitigate biases in AI systems and ensures that the solutions developed are inclusive and equitable. Developing an ecosystem strategy for AI is equally important. It involves recognizing that AI does not exist in a vacuum and that success often requires a network of partnerships and platforms. By engaging with technology partners, academia, startups, and industry groups, organizations can stay at the forefront of AI developments and incorporate external innovations efficiently.

Finally, using AI to facilitate organizational learning turns a company into a learning organization that continuously adapts and evolves based on data-driven insights. AI can reveal patterns in customer behavior, operational inefficiencies, or emerging market trends, which management can then use to refine strategies and processes. In this way, AI becomes a tool not just for automation or analysis, but for continuous improvement at the organizational level.

When these habits are deeply embedded in an organization's culture and operations, they pave the way for transformative growth. The organization becomes nimbler, more responsive to changes, and better equipped to tackle new challenges. By becoming truly AI-savvy, a company does not merely adopt new technology; it reshapes its strategic vision and daily practices to thrive in the digital age. Importantly, aligning AI initiatives with the organization's broader goals and values is not a one-time project but a dynamic, ongoing process. It requires regular reflection and adjustment as both the organization and AI capabilities evolve. In essence, cultivating these five habits is part of a broader commitment to innovation, operational excellence, and strategic growth. Organizations that maintain this commitment are likely to achieve sustained success and a lasting positive impact in their industry and society.

Chapter 3

AI in an organizational context

Rethinking the organization

The adaptive turn in AI: Towards an AI-first view

Adopting an AI-first approach is transformative for organizational leadership. Managers with this mindset proactively integrate AI into the core of their strategies, operations, and cultures. They envision AI not just as a tool, but as a collaborator that complements human ingenuity, driving innovation and efficiency. By embedding AI deeply into organizational practices, leaders can advance their capabilities, making strategic decisions informed by AI's predictive analytics and insights. At the same time, the pursuit of an AI-integrated future must be balanced with ethical considerations, ensuring decisions are made with fairness and transparency. As such, the collaboration between managers and researchers is crucial to develop responsible AI frameworks that uphold these values in the digital landscape, maintaining trust and integrity as organizations evolve with these technologies.

What is an AI-first view then? Before we begin addressing this, we will explore the digital first view. The digital first idea is a strategic approach that prioritizes the development, adoption, and integration of digital technologies, with a strong emphasis on AI and machine learning, as essential drivers of an organization's competitiveness and innovation (Baskerville et al., 2020). This mindset acknowledges the critical role that digital technologies play in today's rapidly evolving market landscape and necessitates a comprehensive transformation of organizational structures, processes, and culture to effectively harness the potential of digital capabilities. In contrast, a "not digital first" view of the organization underestimates the importance of digital technologies and their impact on business operations, competitiveness, and growth. Organizations with this mindset may not prioritize the adoption of digital technologies, resulting in a slower pace of innovation, reduced operational efficiency, and a diminished ability to adapt to changing market dynamics. Instead of embracing digital transformation and investing in data-driven decision-making, digital technology integration, talent management, and ethical considerations, these organizations may continue to rely on traditional business practices and strategies, ultimately hindering their ability to thrive in the digital age.

DOI: 10.4324/9781003733881-3

The "digital first" and "AI-first" paradigms, while intertwined, orient organizations around differing focal points in their strategic embrace of technology. A digital first approach adopts a broad spectrum perspective, emphasizing the integration of all digital technologies as foundational to an organization's strategy. This includes not only AI and machine learning but also other technologies like cloud computing, mobile platforms, and IoT (Internet of Things). The goal is to digitize all aspects of the organization's operations to enhance efficiency, customer experience, and innovation. The organization that adopts a digital first approach sees technology as a tool to support its business strategy and operational processes, regardless of whether AI is a component of the technology. In contrast, an AI-first view is more specialized, placing AI and machine learning at the core of business strategy. Here, AI is not just one of many digital tools but is the primary driver and enabler of the organization's products, services, and internal processes. An AI-first company believes that AI's predictive power and automation capabilities are central to gaining a competitive advantage. This approach invests heavily in AI technologies, talent, and resources, often leading to a radical restructuring around these capabilities to unlock new value propositions and transform business models.

While both views recognize the transformative power of technology, the AI-first perspective goes a step further by positioning AI as the linchpin of future growth and the main catalyst for creating new market opportunities and achieving strategic goals. The digital first idea asserts that information systems are not just mere reflections of the physical world, but rather, they actively shape and create it. Baskerville et al. (2020) postulated that information systems have transcended their role as mere mirrors of physical reality and are now actively molding and defining it. This paradigm shift suggests that in our progressively digitized world, digital renditions of reality are constructed before their physical counterparts, if the latter are deemed necessary.

To adapt to an "AI-first" perspective, managers must adopt a more comprehensive view of the AI landscape. They must understand that user experiences and their computational manifestations cannot be examined in isolation, just as individual organizations' AI systems cannot be scrutinized independently. These systems are increasingly interconnected with multiple platforms, abiding by diverse institutional principles, all of which are in a state of perpetual evolution. Embracing this "AI-first" approach to AI management also necessitates managers to broaden their stakeholder engagement beyond the IT department. It is crucial to include new stakeholders, such as domain experts from a wide array of fields, in the consideration.

With AI technologies at the forefront of digital innovation, the ontological reversal – the idea that digital renditions of reality are constructed before their physical counterparts – suggests that digital takes precedence in shaping our understanding and experiences of reality. As a result, it necessitates a reevaluation of the role of humans, technology, and information systems in society, as well as the responsibilities of scholars seeking to understand the role of AI in organizations and society.

In an AI-first world, AI technologies play a central role in transforming the way we interact with our environment, make decisions, and solve problems. These advanced systems not only automate processes but also augment human capabilities, enabling organizations to leverage the power of AI in creating new products, services, and experiences that were previously unimaginable. The increasing pervasiveness of AI also raises critical ethical concerns, such as privacy, security, and fairness, which must be addressed in the design, implementation, and governance of these technologies.

Embracing the AI-first idea entails adopting a holistic perspective that considers the complex and dynamic interplay between humans, technology, and society. In particular, the focus should extend beyond individual information systems and user experiences to examine the broader socio-technical ecosystem in which AI and other digital technologies operate. This ecosystem comprises multiple platforms, stakeholders, and institutional logics that continually evolve and influence one another.

By adopting an AI-first mindset, managers can better understand and address the challenges and opportunities presented by AI and other digital technologies. This may involve investigating new ways to integrate AI into business processes, exploring innovative human-AI collaboration models, and examining the ethical implications of AI-driven decision-making. Moreover, the AI-first idea calls for a reevaluation of the traditional boundaries between the digital and physical worlds. As AI continues to blur these lines, managers must adapt their thinking to account for the increasingly intertwined nature of our digital and physical experiences.

The AI-first idea emphasizes the need for a more comprehensive and integrated approach to the study of AI systems and their role in shaping our reality. For scholars as well as practitioners, it is crucial to recognize the evolving nature of the socio-technical ecosystem and adapt our research focus accordingly, to better understand and harness the transformative potential of AI and other digital technologies. The AI-first approach implies that organizations must prioritize the development, adoption, and integration of digital technologies, with a strong emphasis on AI and machine learning, to maintain their competitiveness and drive innovation. This view of the organization recognizes that digital technologies have become essential for businesses to thrive in today's rapidly evolving market landscape. To achieve an AI-first mindset, organizations need to consider several key factors when implementing AI in their operations and strategies.

Digital transformation: To effectively incorporate AI into their business models, organizations need to undergo a digital transformation that involves rethinking their organizational structures, processes, and culture. This includes investing in the necessary infrastructure, such as cloud computing and data storage, to support the development and deployment of AI applications. Additionally, organizations should promote a digital first culture that encourages collaboration, experimentation, and agility, enabling them to quickly adapt to new market trends and technologies.

Data-driven decision-making: AI and machine learning thrive on data, and the digital first approach emphasizes the importance of leveraging data to inform strategic decisions. Organizations should invest in robust data management systems and analytics tools that enable them to collect, store, and analyze vast amounts of data. This will allow organizations to gain valuable insights and make data-driven decisions.

AI integration: Organizations must thoughtfully integrate AI technologies into their core business processes and operations. This entails identifying areas where AI can add the most value, such as automating repetitive tasks, augmenting human decision-making, or personalizing customer experiences. Successful AI integration requires a clear understanding of the organization's goals, as well as the capabilities and limitations of AI technologies.

Talent management and upskilling: To harness the potential of AI, organizations need to invest in acquiring and developing the right talent. This includes hiring skilled AI professionals, such as data scientists and machine learning engineers, and providing ongoing training and development opportunities for existing employees.

Collaboration and partnerships: The AI-first approach also involves forging strategic partnerships and collaborations with other organizations, such as technology vendors, academic institutions, and industry consortia. These collaborations can facilitate knowledge sharing, access to cutting-edge AI technologies, and the development of best practices for AI implementation.

The AI-first idea emphasizes the need for organizations to prioritize the development and integration of AI technologies to remain competitive. By focusing on digital transformation, data-driven decision-making, AI integration, talent management, ethical considerations, and strategic collaborations, organizations can successfully adopt a digital first mindset and harness the full potential of AI to drive growth and innovation. The digital first view of the organization suggests that organizations must prioritize digital capabilities in order to remain competitive. This means that organizations must embrace new technologies such as AI and machine learning in order to stay ahead of the curve. Organizations that are able to effectively harness the power of digital technologies will be better positioned to gain a competitive advantage in the marketplace.

The integration of AI into an organization's operations represents a shift towards a digital first view. The classical view of an information system is that it represents and reflects physical reality, but with the advent of AI, this view is becoming increasingly obsolete. The digital first view of the organization suggests that organizations must prioritize digital capabilities to remain competitive. This view holds that digital technologies, such as AI, are increasingly becoming a key driver of organizational performance and that organizations must develop digital capabilities to remain competitive. This perspective has several implications for AI management.

First, it highlights the importance of investing in AI as a strategic capability. Organizations that adopt a digital first view must recognize that AI is a key enabler of digital transformation and that it is a key driver of organizational performance. This means that organizations must invest in AI as a strategic capability, which means investing in the necessary infrastructure, talent, and data.

Second, the AI-first view implies that organizations must prioritize data as a key asset. Organizations that adopt a digital first view must recognize that data is the fuel that powers AI and that it is a key asset. This means that organizations must prioritize data as a key asset and invest in data management and governance capabilities to ensure that data is accurate, complete, and timely.

Third, the AI-first view implies that organizations must focus on the customer experience. Organizations that adopt a digital first view must recognize that the customer experience is becoming increasingly digital, and that AI can be used to improve the customer experience. This means that organizations must focus on using AI to improve the customer experience and invest in customer experience management capabilities.

The adoption of an AI-first perspective within organizations carries profound consequences for the management of AI, underscoring the need to recognize AI as a key strategic resource. It necessitates an organization-wide reassessment of data as an invaluable asset, placing a spotlight on refining customer interactions. As such, by integrating an AI-first approach and elevating the importance of AI, data handling, and customer experience, businesses can drive meaningful value creation.

Towards an ecosystem view of AI

Today, AI does not exist in isolation; rather, it thrives within vast, interconnected ecosystems. This concept of ecosystems in AI mirrors the biological analogy where diverse entities share a space and potentially overlap, creating an intricate web of relationships that may be symbiotic or competitive, fostering growth or leading to decline. Indeed, AI in the modern context operates much like organisms within a biological ecosystem, where its growth and functionality are deeply interlinked with various elements of the environment it inhabits. AI systems interact with a multitude of actors, processes, and other technologies, forming a network of relationships that are dynamic and may be mutually beneficial or competitive. The health and evolution of this ecosystem depend on how well these interactions are managed, with the potential for AI to either drive innovation and progress or lead to inefficiencies and setbacks. Understanding and navigating this AI ecosystem is crucial for leveraging its capabilities to the fullest.

These ecosystems comprise not just AI technologies but also humans, organizations, policies, and the environment, all interacting in a complex, dynamic dance. In this context, the ecosystem view becomes indispensable. It allows us to understand AI not as a series of standalone innovations but as a collective entity that operates within and influences a broader context. The actors within these ecosystems – whether individuals, communities, organizations, or technologies – do not merely exist alongside one another but engage in a continuous exchange, affecting and being affected by the ecosystem's shifting conditions.

The ecosystem view provides a robust conceptual foundation that aids in grasping the multifaceted social reality of intelligent systems. However, the ecosystem metaphor also introduces profound ethical quandaries. When considering AI as part of an ecosystem, the question arises: who, or what, bears the moral responsibility for the actions and consequences of this collective? Traditional ethical frameworks falter when applied to such a complex system where agency is dispersed and not easily pinpointed.

The ecosystem view suggests that AI should be understood as an "ecosystem of ecosystems," a network of interrelated systems each defined by unique artifacts, locations, and members. This perspective offers an appreciation of AI's consequences observed in the real world, which often transcend individual technical artifacts or entities. Yet, this metaphorical ecosystem cannot itself be held accountable. The requirements for ascribing responsibility – such as awareness and the ability to effect change – are attributes not easily associated with a socio-technical ecosystem. The challenge then becomes one of conceptualization: How can we imagine a responsible ecosystem of intelligent systems? What does accountability look like in this vast, interconnected space?

To address these challenges, we must envision a new framework for responsibility within AI ecosystems. This framework would need to acknowledge the distributed nature of agency and the emergent properties of complex systems. It would also have to consider the diverse actors within the ecosystem, their varying degrees of influence, and the potential for collective decision-making processes. As such, the ecosystem view of AI is not merely a metaphor but a critical lens through which the breadth and depth of AI's impact on society can be understood. It prompts us to reconsider how we approach the design, development, and governance of AI systems.

AI has the potential to fundamentally change the way organizations operate and compete. One of the most significant changes that AI may bring is the shift from an organization-centric view to a network-centric view. This change is driven by the growing importance of AI ecosystems, which are networks of organizations and individuals that collaborate to create and deliver AI-based products and services. In essence, the vanishing organization is not disappearing in the literal sense but is transforming from a fixed, rigid structure into a dynamic, fluid network. It is a reflection of how modern organizations are adapting to the digital age, harnessing the power of AI and the global economy to redefine what an organization looks like and how it operates.

Traditionally, organizations have focused on building internal capabilities to create and deliver products and services. This organization-centric view assumes that organizations are the primary actors in the economy and that they can create value by developing and controlling their own resources. However, the emergence of AI has challenged this assumption by making it increasingly difficult for organizations to create and control all the resources they need to compete. The growing complexity and rapid pace of technological change in AI have made it difficult for organizations to keep up with the latest developments and maintain a competitive edge. As a result, organizations are increasingly turning to external partners to access the resources and expertise they need to develop and deliver AI-based products and services. This shift from an organization-centric view to a network-centric view is driven by the growing importance of AI ecosystems. An AI ecosystem is a network of organizations and individuals that collaborate to create and deliver AI-based products and services. It includes a wide range of actors, such as technology providers, data providers, system integrators, and end-users. Each actor plays a unique role in the ecosystem and contributes to its overall success. For example, technology providers develop and supply the AI technologies and tools that are used to develop and deliver AI-based products and services. Data providers supply the data that is used to train and test AI models. System integrators help organizations to implement and deploy AI-based products and services. End-users are the organizations and individuals that use AI-based products and services to improve their operations and create new products and services.

The emergence of AI ecosystems has led to a shift in the way organizations create and deliver value. In the past, organizations were focused on creating value by controlling their own resources and capabilities. However, in an AI ecosystem, organizations can create value by collaborating with other actors to access the resources and expertise they need to develop and deliver AI-based products and services. For example, a company that specializes in manufacturing may not have the resources or expertise to develop and deploy an AI-based product. However, by collaborating with a technology provider, a data provider, and a system integrator, the manufacturing company can access the resources and expertise it needs to develop and deploy an AI-based product. This collaboration enables the manufacturing company to create value by using AI to improve its operations and create new products and services.

The shift from an organization-centric view to a network-centric view is also driven by the changing nature of competition in the AI market. In the past, organizations competed primarily with other organizations in their industry. However, in an AI ecosystem, organizations compete with a wide range of actors, including other organizations in their industry, technology providers, data providers, system integrators, and end-users. This competition is driven by the growing importance of data and AI technologies in creating value. For example, a technology provider may compete with other technology providers to supply AI technologies and tools to organizations. A data provider may compete with other data providers to supply data to organizations. A system integrator may compete with other system integrators to help organizations implement and deploy AI-based products and services. An end-user may compete with other end-users to create the most innovative and valuable AI-based products and services.

The shift from an organization-centric view to a network-centric view, driven by the increasing importance of AI, has significant implications for organizations and industries. An organization-centric view assumes that organizations are the primary actors in the economy and that they can create value by developing and controlling their own resources. However, the emergence of AI has challenged this assumption by making it increasingly difficult for organizations to create and control all the resources they need to compete. The growing complexity and rapid pace of technological change in AI have made it necessary for organizations to turn to external partners for resources and expertise to develop and deliver AI-based products and services. This shift to a network-centric view is driven by the growing importance of AI ecosystems.

An AI ecosystem is a network of organizations and individuals that collaborate to create and deliver AI-based products and services. It includes a wide range of actors, such as technology providers, data providers, system integrators, and end-users. Each actor plays a unique role in the ecosystem and contributes to its overall success. The emergence of AI ecosystems has led to a shift in the way organizations create and deliver value. In the past, organizations were focused on creating value by controlling their own resources and capabilities. However, in an AI ecosystem, organizations can create value by collaborating with other actors to access the resources and expertise they need to develop and deliver AI-based products and services.

The shift to a network-centric view has several implications for organizations. First, it requires organizations to be more open and collaborative. In a network-centric view, organizations need to be willing to share data and expertise with other actors in the ecosystem to create value. This means that organizations need to establish trust and build relationships with other actors in the ecosystem. Second, the shift to a network-centric view requires organizations to be more agile and adaptable. In a network-centric view, organizations need to be able to quickly respond to changes in the ecosystem and adapt their strategies accordingly. This requires organizations to have the ability to quickly access and leverage new resources and expertise as they become available. Third, the shift to a network-centric view requires organizations to be more focused on creating value for customers. In a network-centric view, organizations need to be more customer-centric and focused on creating value for end-users. This requires organizations to have a deep understanding of customer needs and to be able to deliver products and services that meet those needs.

The rise of AI has precipitated a paradigm shift from traditional, inward-looking organizational frameworks to expansive, network-centric models. In this new landscape, the ability of an organization to form and maintain a web of partnerships and collaborations becomes a critical asset. Such a network-centric view harnesses collective capabilities and fosters innovation through shared knowledge and resources. This transition entails a cultural shift within organizations, which must become more open to sharing data and insights while protecting their intellectual property and customer privacy. It also demands a willingness to engage in collaborative ventures that may have been unthinkable in a more siloed past.

Agility and adaptability are further hallmarks of this shift. In a fast-moving AI-driven economy, the ability to pivot in response to new information and rapidly evolving market conditions is invaluable. AI can aid in this by providing real-time insights and forecasts, enabling organizations to make informed decisions swiftly. Moreover, a focus on creating value for customers is amplified in a network-centric model. Organizations can leverage AI to gain a deeper understanding of customer needs and behaviors, allowing for more personalized experiences and innovative service offerings. By utilizing AI to analyze trends and patterns, organizations can anticipate customer needs, sometimes even before the customers themselves are aware of them.

Organizations adept at navigating this shift are likely to find themselves at a competitive advantage. They will not only optimize their internal operations but also play a central role in shaping the ecosystems in which they operate. The network-centric approach breaks down barriers, allowing for a more fluid exchange of ideas and solutions that can drive collective success. In an AI-driven economy, the most successful organizations will be those that view AI not as a tool for automating processes but as a transformative force that can redefine the very essence of how they operate and deliver value. It is a move towards a more interconnected and intelligent business environment, where the boundaries between an organization and its network are not barriers but bridges to innovation and growth.

Managing the AI organization: Towards an adaptive view

As organizations integrate AI systems into their operations, it is becoming increasingly important for managers and leaders to understand how to effectively manage these systems. A key for the AI organization, in this context, is the integration of AI and human workers, and it is crucial for managers to understand how to effectively manage and optimize the performance of these systems. This includes understanding the strengths and limitations of AI systems, as well as developing strategies for effectively integrating them with human workers.

AI, particularly generative AI, is a technology that has the potential to significantly impact both digital innovation and digital transformation. Generative AI involves the use of algorithms and neural networks to create new data and content, such as images, videos, and text. One of the ways that generative AI blurs the lines between digital innovation and digital transformation is by creating new opportunities for businesses to innovate and create value for customers. For example, a company may use generative AI to create personalized products, content, and experiences that are tailored to individual customer preferences. At the same time, generative AI can also play a role in digital transformation by enabling businesses to automate and optimize their operations. For example, a company may use generative AI to automate repetitive tasks, improve supply chain efficiency, or enhance customer service. However, navigating this complex landscape requires a strategic approach that considers the potential risks and challenges associated with AI. For example, businesses must consider issues related to data privacy, ethical concerns, and potential biases that may arise in the use of AI algorithms.

In recent years, the field of AI has undergone an "adaptive turn," shifting the emphasis from conceptualizing AI algorithms to understanding how these algorithms are continuously adapted and applied in practice. In early AI strategy research, the focus was on the structural *control view*, which emphasized the installation and operation of changes called for in a strategic plan. The goal was to control performance with respect to desired ends, and this was to be achieved through a series of interventions concerning organizational structures, key personnel actions, and control systems. This control view assumed a deterministic approach to strategy implementation, where the focus was on the operationalization of a predefined strategic plan, and the role of organizational actors was seen as limited to the execution of the plan.

However, with the increased diffusion of AI in organizational settings, a more *adaptive view* of strategy implementation has gained prominence. This adaptive view recognizes that the use of AI systems in organizations is not a one-way street where AI shapes organizational practices, but rather a two-way street where both AI and organizational practices mutually shape each other (Lindgren & Holmström, 2020). In this view, strategy implementation is defined as the communication, interpretation, adoption, and enactment of strategic plans. This definition reflects an adaptive approach, where strategy implementation is seen as a process of sensemaking, learning, and adaptation, rather than a mechanical process of executing a predefined plan.

The control view of strategy implementation assumes that organizational practices can be controlled and optimized through the use of AI systems. The focus is on the design and implementation of AI systems that can help organizations achieve their desired ends by automating tasks, reducing errors, and improving efficiency. This view sees AI as a tool for achieving predetermined outcomes, and the role of organizational actors is seen as limited to the execution of tasks assigned to them by the AI system.

In contrast, the adaptation view recognizes that AI systems are not neutral tools that can be used to control and optimize organizational practices. Rather, AI systems are shaped by organizational practices, and organizational practices are shaped by the use of AI systems. In this view, AI systems are seen as co-constructive agents that interact with organizational actors to shape organizational practices. The focus is on the co-creation of value, where AI systems and organizational actors work together to achieve desired outcomes.

The control view assumes a deterministic approach to strategy implementation, where the focus is on the operationalization of a predefined strategic plan. The role of organizational actors is seen as limited to the execution of tasks assigned to them by the AI system. In contrast, the adaptation view recognizes the importance of sensemaking and learning in strategy implementation. The focus is on the interpretation and enactment of strategic plans, and the role of organizational actors is seen as active agents in the process of sensemaking, learning, and adaptation. The control view also assumes that AI systems are objective and neutral tools that can be used to optimize organizational practices. However, the adaptation view recognizes that AI systems are not neutral and objective but are embedded in social and cultural contexts. AI systems are shaped by the values, norms, and practices of the organization in which they are used, and they, in turn, shape organizational practices by influencing the way organizational actors make sense of their work. In addition, the control view assumes that the use of AI systems can lead to a reduction in the need for human labor, as tasks are automated and optimized. However, the adaptation view recognizes that the use of AI systems can also lead to the creation of new forms of work and new roles for organizational actors. AI systems can enable new forms of collaboration and coordination, as well as new forms of creativity and innovation.

The distinction between the control view and the adaptation view in AI research and practice highlights the importance of recognizing that the use of AI systems in organizational settings is not a one-way street where AI shapes organizational practices but rather a two-way street where both AI and organizational practices mutually shape each other. The control view assumes a deterministic approach to strategy implementation, where the focus is on the operationalization of a predefined strategic plan.

AI has the potential to fundamentally change the way organizations operate and compete. As noted above, the shift from an organization-centric view to a network-centric view, driven by the increasing importance of AI, has significant

Table 3.1 The control view and the adaptation view in AI research and practice

	Role of agency	Role of AI technology	Role of AI strategy
Control view	Top management as formulators and middle management as implementors of strategy	Focus on structures, incentives, and controls as the main coordinating mechanisms	Focus on conceptualization of strategies, structures and implementation plans
Adaptive view	Middle and lower-level managers as active participants in the strategy implementation process	Focus on sense-giving, rhetoric, talk and text, and discourse as coordinating mechanisms	Focus on organizational enacting of strategy in the actions and interactions of organizational members

implications for how organizations should be managed. An organization-centric view assumes that organizations are the primary actors in the economy and that they can create value by developing and controlling their own resources. However, the emergence of AI has challenged this assumption by making it increasingly difficult for organizations to create and control all the resources they need to compete. The growing complexity and rapid pace of technological change in AI have made it necessary for organizations to turn to external partners for resources and expertise to develop and deliver AI-based products and services. This shift to a network-centric view is driven by the growing importance of AI ecosystems.

To effectively manage an AI organization in a network-centric view, organizations need to focus on four key areas: strategy, organization, culture, and talent. First, organizations need to develop a clear and comprehensive AI strategy. This strategy should be aligned with the overall business strategy and should consider the organization's current capabilities, resources, and expertise. Organizations also need to be aware of the latest trends and developments in AI and how they can be leveraged to create value. Second, organizations need to reorganize their internal structures to better align with the network-centric view. This means creating cross-functional teams that are responsible for developing and delivering AI-based products and services. Organizations also need to establish partnerships and collaborations with other actors in the ecosystem, such as technology providers, data providers, and system integrators. Third, organizations need to foster a culture that is conducive to the network-centric view. This means creating a culture of openness, collaboration, and innovation. Organizations need to encourage employees to share data and expertise with other actors in the ecosystem and to be open to new ideas and ways of working. Lastly, organizations need to attract and retain the talent that is necessary to successfully compete in an AI-driven economy. This means investing in the training and development of employees and creating an environment that is conducive to the retention of top talent.

The shift from an organization-centric view to a network-centric view, driven by the increasing importance of AI, has significant implications for how organizations should be managed. Organizations need to focus on developing a clear and comprehensive AI strategy, reorganizing their internal structures, fostering a culture that is conducive to the network-centric view, and attracting and retaining the talent that is necessary to successfully compete in an AI-driven economy. Today, organizations that do not prioritize AI in their strategic planning may find themselves at a competitive disadvantage. Adopting an AI-first view is not merely about leveraging new technology but about fundamentally reimagining the role of traditional business processes in light of AI's capabilities.

Traditionally, the focal firm has been at the center of its business universe, with suppliers and customers orbiting around it. However, as AI ecosystems grow in importance, the boundaries of the focal firm begin to blur. AI ecosystems are collaborative networks that transcend traditional industry boundaries, integrating various stakeholders including technology providers, developers, users, and even competitors into a synergistic whole. As AI ecosystems become a critical driver of value creation and innovation, they allow for the sharing of data, algorithms, and insights, which can accelerate the development and adoption of AI across different sectors. Organizations that do not engage with these ecosystems risk being isolated from the cutting-edge advancements and the collective intelligence that these ecosystems foster. As AI ecosystems expand, the idea of a single, focal firm dominating a market is becoming outdated. Instead, value is created through collaboration and integration across different players within the ecosystem. The organizations that succeed will be those that can position themselves as integral parts of these broader ecosystems, leveraging the collective capabilities and insights to drive innovation and strategic advantage.

The adaptive view of AI involves a focus on the organizational enacting of strategy in the actions and interactions of organizational members. This highlights a continuous and evolving process where strategy emerges from the collective actions and interactions within the organization rather than being dictated from above. As such, the steps towards an AI-first view indicate a shift towards a more dynamic, inclusive, and flexible approach to AI in organizations. The adaptive view suggests that organizations are increasingly recognizing the value of harnessing the collective intelligence and adaptability of their members, facilitated by AI, to navigate the complexities of the modern business environment. This view aligns with the emergent nature of strategy and the increasing pace of change, requiring organizations to be more responsive and adaptable. Against this backdrop, the necessity for organizations to adopt an AI-first view is clear. It allows for a more nimble, efficient, and customer-centric approach to business. Furthermore, the rise of AI ecosystems signifies a shift away from the traditional focal firm model towards a more distributed, collaborative, and integrated approach to creating value.

Chapter 4

AI readiness

What is AI readiness and why is it important?

Today, AI has emerged as a transformative force, reshaping industries, redefining operational paradigms, and offering unprecedented opportunities for innovation and growth. The advent of advanced AI technologies has brought forth a new era where data-driven decision-making and automation have become key determinants of organizational success. However, the ability to harness the full potential of AI extends beyond mere adoption; it necessitates a comprehensive readiness strategy that prepares organizations to navigate the complexities and challenges inherent in integrating AI into their core functions. This chapter focuses on the concept of "AI readiness" – a multifaceted approach that equips organizations to effectively leverage AI capabilities – ensuring they are poised to capitalize on the promises and advantages that advanced AI offers.

AI readiness is not merely a technological upgrade but a strategic imperative that encompasses cultural, operational, ethical, and skill-related dimensions. In an era where AI is set to become a critical driver of competitive advantage, organizations must cultivate a conducive ecosystem that fosters innovation, supports continuous learning, and promotes ethical AI use. The significance of AI readiness is underscored by the rapid pace of technological advancements and the increasing complexity of AI systems, which demand a proactive approach to governance, talent development, and infrastructure readiness. This chapter aims to underscore the importance of AI readiness, outlining the key components and strategic considerations that organizations must address to thrive in an AI-driven future, thereby enabling them to not only adapt to the changing technological landscape but also to shape it.

AI readiness has become a critical aspect for organizations aiming to stay competitive and innovative. Being AI-ready is not just about adopting new technologies but cultivating a holistic environment where AI can thrive and drive meaningful outcomes. This entails developing capabilities that span across technical infrastructure, workforce skills, and strategic vision, ensuring that organizations are equipped to leverage AI effectively.

DOI: 10.4324/9781003733881-4

Having the necessary capabilities requires a workforce that is not only skilled in using AI tools but is also adaptable to new ways of working that these technologies bring. This involves continuous learning and development programs that empower employees to harness AI in their roles.

Resources are equally crucial, extending beyond financial investments to include access to quality data, which is the lifeblood of any AI system. A reliable and diverse dataset is paramount for training AI algorithms to perform accurately and ethically. Moreover, having a network of external partners and collaborators can provide additional expertise and insights, which are often necessary for the development and scaling of AI initiatives. Lastly, the mindset shift towards AI readiness is perhaps the most significant change. It encompasses a cultural transformation where every level of the organization embraces innovation and is prepared to rethink traditional processes and business models. This forward-thinking mindset also involves a readiness to navigate the ethical implications of AI, ensuring that AI solutions are developed and deployed responsibly.

AI readiness transcends the mere technical deployment of AI applications; it is about building a foundation where AI is interwoven into the organizational fabric, driving decision-making, innovation, and operational efficiency. As AI continues to redefine what is possible, being AI-ready allows organizations to harness its full potential, adapt to changes, and create value in an increasingly complex and data-driven world. The AI readiness framework provides organizations with a structured approach to assess their preparedness for adopting and implementing AI technologies (Holmström, 2022). The framework helps organizations understand their current situation, identify gaps, and develop strategies to move forward in their AI journey. The AI readiness framework is composed of four key dimensions that organizations should consider: technologies, activities, boundaries, and goals. By evaluating these dimensions, organizations can gain a comprehensive understanding of their AI readiness, identify areas for improvement, and develop strategies to address these gaps. The AI readiness framework thus provides a valuable tool for organizations to navigate the complex and dynamic landscape of AI adoption, ensuring they are well-prepared to harness the potential benefits of AI while minimizing potential risks and challenges.

The journey towards AI readiness, however, does not only entail these steps; it also entails measuring the current level of AI readiness for an organization. Holmström (2022) provides insights for organizations on how to adapt AI in their organization and create value from it. Specifically, it outlines a framework for how to measure the level of AI readiness for an organization. The imperative of AI readiness cannot be overstated, as it provides a clear roadmap for organizations to not just adopt AI but to maximize its potential. Measuring AI readiness becomes critical in this context – it is an assessment of an organization's current state against a set of criteria that are essential for successful AI integration. At the core of the AI readiness framework, which emerged from a series of workshops with a diverse set of organizations, is the idea that AI transformation is more than a technological shift; it is a strategic evolution.

The workshops that gave rise to the AI readiness framework were collaborative efforts, drawing insights from leaders in various fields, and synthesizing best practices across industries. The framework is holistic, taking into account the technological infrastructure, the availability of data, the skills of the workforce, the organization's cultural readiness to embrace change, and the ethical implications of deploying AI. The importance of this framework lies in its ability to identify gaps and provide targeted strategies to mitigate them, ensuring that organizations are not only prepared to implement AI but are also resilient and agile enough to evolve with AI advancements. It is a tool for organizations to benchmark their progress, develop a clear strategy, and systematically approach the adoption of AI, thus fostering a culture of innovation and securing a competitive edge in the rapidly advancing technological landscape.

To assess the AI readiness of an organization, it is crucial to define AI readiness as the organization's ability to deploy and use AI in ways that add value to the organization. Using the AI readiness framework, managers should assess and visualize the four key dimensions of readiness, which are technologies, activities, boundaries, and goals. This framework can be applied in workshop settings to allow organization members to grade their organization's capabilities, both current and future potential, in each dimension. This approach can help managers highlight the risks and challenges involved in digital transformation associated with organization-wide mobilization of AI technologies for new ends, which often have low success rates. By utilizing the multi-dimensional AI readiness framework as a pragmatic tool, managers can facilitate efforts to meet the associated challenges, reduce the risks, and increase success rates. The framework should be used as a tool to identify where the organization stands in terms of AI readiness and to identify areas that need improvement to boost the adoption of AI and reap its benefits.

The AI readiness framework can be used to enable the capture and tracing of an organization's socio-technological AI status, to assist the characterization of associated cultural factors, and to facilitate efforts to address key bottlenecks. This framework focuses on four key dimensions of organizational life: technologies, activities, boundaries, and goals. These dimensions are considered separately for clarity, but they are interdependent (see Figure 4.1). The framework can be applied in a workshop setting, where an organization's management team can use a self-reporting questionnaire to assess the organization's AI readiness.

The dimension of technologies is closely related to the functional qualities of digital technologies and how they shape the organization's activities, boundaries, and goals. The dimension of activities relates to how algorithm-governed digital systems can enable organizations to perform activities more effectively and to augment their capacities. The dimension of boundaries relates to how

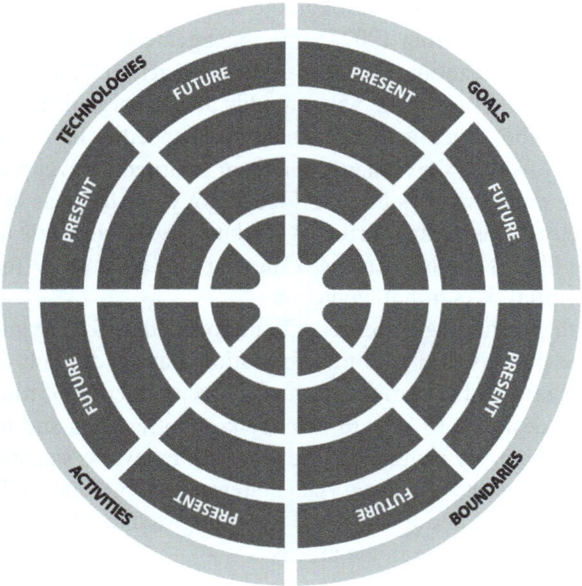

Figure 4.1 AI Readiness Scorecard

digital transformation can reshape occupational boundaries. The dimension of goals relates to how organizations can use AI to achieve their goals and how AI can help to shape their future goals. We will elaborate on each dimension in the coming sections.

AI readiness dimension #1: Technologies

The first AI readiness dimension to consider is technology. As a manager, it is important to understand the impact of digital technologies on your organization and the nature of work. Recent advances in digital technologies have led to large-scale transformations of occupations, job roles, and entire industries. One way to assess the readiness of your organization to adopt and leverage these technologies is by using the AI readiness framework. This framework can be applied in a workshop setting, where your management team can use a self-reporting questionnaire to assess the organization's current and future AI technology portfolio (see questionnaire in Appendix 1).

An important aspect to consider when assessing the technology dimension of the framework is the functional qualities of digital technologies, such as editability and generativity. These qualities shape the organization's activities, boundaries, and goals (Alaimo et al., 2020) and can have a significant impact on the organization's ability to create value through the use of AI. For example, in a case study presented in Holmström (2022), the management team of an insurance firm awarded the organization a score of 4 (excellent) for their current AI technology portfolio in terms of the value it adds to their organization. This portfolio included a chatbot function and data analytics capacities based on TensorFlow and Tableau. However, the management team awarded a lower rating of 2 (moderate) for the organization's future AI technology portfolio, as the organization had no strategy for using any further AI technology to add value to the organization. This highlights the importance of having a clear strategy for leveraging AI and the potential risks of not having one.

It is important to note that technology alone is difficult to evaluate for organizational members, and the process of digital transformation may be difficult to achieve, as it takes place against a background of the daily reproduction of routines, so the framework is designed to help to identify key bottlenecks and to facilitate efforts to address them. By using the AI readiness framework, starting by considering the role of technology, managers can better understand the readiness of their organization to adopt and leverage AI technologies and take steps to address any challenges that may arise in the process.

AI readiness dimension #2: Activities

The second AI readiness dimension is the set of activities AI may be implicated in. As a manager, it is important to understand the impact of AI systems on your organization's ability to perform activities more effectively and to augment their capacities. However, it is important to note that these systems also have affordances that can have radically differing consequences from planned changes. Additionally, they can also organize, manage, and control many activities delegated to them by humans, but this control is not always obvious or transparent.

Continuing with the case study presented in Holmström (2022), after appraising the insurance organization's technological status, the management team considered the activities dimension and awarded the organization a score of 2 (moderate) in terms of its AI's value-adding support for key activities. The activities supported by AI technology at the time of the assessment were customer support and data analytics. Although there were no concrete plans to expand these activities or to push for deeper use of AI, there was some evidence of enthusiasm for expansion in the future, as a score of 3 (high) was awarded for the organization's strategies for supporting future activities with AI.

Interestingly, the insurance organization evaluated their AI readiness related to activities lower than their AI readiness related to technologies. As a manager, in the insurance organization and elsewhere, it is important to be aware of the potential impact of digital transformation on the organization's activities and to be prepared to adapt to changes and to take advantage of the opportunities they present.

Using the AI readiness framework can help you to identify key areas where the organization can leverage AI to improve its activities and plan for the future.

AI readiness dimension #3: Boundaries

The third AI readiness dimension to consider is the set of boundaries that are implicated in the digital transformation processes. As a manager, it is important to understand the impact of digital transformation on organizational boundaries. Changes that occur in digital transformation may involve expansion, contraction, or even disappearance of boundaries. This can happen due to organizations establishing new digital innovation units, layoffs of organizational members, and skill replacements. Additionally, boundaries may also change as physical products are increasingly enhanced with digital components, such as sensors, or as linear value creation is dissolved through the incorporation of digital capabilities that allow for the addition of novel services during their life cycles.

Continuing with the case study presented by Holmström (2022), the management team considered boundaries as the third dimension of AI readiness and awarded the organization a score of just 1 (low) on the 0–4 scale for value-adding changes in organizational boundaries associated with the use of AI. The team mentioned only a few examples of boundary-stretching such as experiments with smart home solutions and the emergence of big, complex, and unstructured data sets from such experiments. However, in the long run, the team believed that the boundaries with customers and real estate owners are likely to change, but current initiatives that could induce or include boundary changes did not extend beyond these experiments. The participants expressed enthusiasm about these experiments and hope that some of the tested ideas will be realized in the future, leading to a self-reported score of 2 (moderate) for value-adding strategies to stretch organizational boundaries using AI in the future. As a whole, the boundary dimension was evaluated as more problematic compared to technologies and activities.

As a manager, it is important to be aware of the potential impact of digital transformation on organizational boundaries and to be prepared to adapt to changes and to take advantage of the opportunities they present. Using the AI readiness framework can help you to identify key areas where the organization can leverage AI to stretch its boundaries and plan for the future.

AI readiness dimension #4: Goals

The fourth and final AI readiness dimension is the set of goals implicated in the digital transformation process. As digital technologies continue to evolve, it is highly important for organizations to assess their AI readiness in order to effectively deploy and use AI in ways that add value to the organization's ultimate goals. Goals, in this context, are related to the strategic aspects of digital transformation. The AI readiness framework is designed to assist in this assessment by focusing not only on the goals but on the four key dimensions of AI readiness for the organization: technologies, activities, boundaries, and goals.

Exploring the case from Holmström (2022), when it comes to technologies, it is important for an organization to have a clear understanding of the value their current AI technology portfolio adds to their organization, as well as their potential for future growth in this area. In the case of the insurance organization assessed in the workshop, the management team gave a score of 4 (excellent) for their current portfolio, but a score of 2 (moderate) for their potential in the future. When it comes to activities, it is important to consider how AI technology is currently supporting key activities within the organization and to have strategies in place for future growth in this area. The insurance organization was given a score of 2 (moderate) in terms of current value-adding support for activities, but a score of 3 (high) for their future strategies. Boundaries are another important aspect to consider, as changes in digital transformation may involve expansion, contraction, or even disappearance of boundaries. In the workshop, the management team gave the insurance organization a score of 1 (low) for value-adding changes in organizational boundaries associated with the use of AI, but a score of 2 (moderate) for future strategies to stretch organizational boundaries using AI. The full scorecard can be found in Figure 4.2.

Lastly, it is important to consider the impact of digital transformation on an organization's goals and identities. The insurance organization was given a score of 0 (none) for present AI use providing value-adding support for attainment of the organization's goals, but a score of 1 (low) for increasing use of AI to provide value-adding support for the organization's goals in the future.

The evaluation reflects how often the goal dimension in the AI readiness framework is the most challenging dimension for organizations. It is important to remember that these dimensions are interdependent and should be considered both separately and holistically when assessing an organization's AI readiness. By focusing on these four key dimensions, organizations can better understand their current and potential capabilities, identify potential challenges and risks, and ultimately increase their chances of success in digital transformation efforts.

It is important to note that the process of digital transformation may be difficult to achieve, as it takes place against a background of the daily reproduction of routines, so the framework is designed to help to identify key bottlenecks and to facilitate efforts to address them. It is also important to remember that this framework is a tool to identify where the organization stands in terms of AI readiness and to identify areas that need improvement to boost the adoption of AI and reap its benefits.

The AI readiness framework also suggests that organizations should focus on creating value from AI, rather than simply implementing it for the sake of it. To do this, organizations need to understand the potential benefits and limitations of AI and identify specific use cases where it can create value. While AI has

Figure 4.2 AI Readiness Scorecard Results

the potential to revolutionize the way organizations operate and create value, organizations need to be ready for AI to fully realize this potential. Being ready for AI involves a number of different elements being in place, including having a clear strategy, investing in the right talent and technology, and addressing the ethical and societal implications of AI.

At the end of the day, one of the most important elements of being ready for AI is having a clear strategy. Organizations need to understand the potential of AI and how it can be used to create value. This requires a deep understanding of the different types of AI, the use cases where AI can be applied, and the potential risks and benefits of AI. With a clear strategy in place, organizations can identify the most valuable use cases for AI and develop a roadmap for how to realize this potential. Another important element of being ready for AI is investing in the right talent and technology. Organizations need to have the right people with the right skills to develop and deploy AI-based solutions. This includes data scientists, engineers, and experts in the social sciences to help understand and address the ethical and societal implications of AI. Organizations also need to invest in the right technology infrastructure to support AI, including data storage, computing power, and the necessary software and tools. Finally, organizations need to be aware of and address the ethical and societal implications of AI. AI has the potential to impact society in many ways, including employment, privacy, and decision-making. Organizations need to be aware of these implications and develop policies and processes to ensure that AI is developed and deployed in a responsible and ethical manner.

To truly unlock the value that AI promises, organizations must adopt a comprehensive view of AI readiness, incorporating technology, activities, boundaries, and goals. These dimensions collectively provide a framework for assessing and enhancing an organization's capacity to implement and benefit from AI. Technologically, readiness involves not only the adoption of advanced AI tools but also the establishment of robust data governance and infrastructure that underpin AI systems. Activities related to AI readiness include the development of processes and workflows that integrate AI capabilities effectively, fostering an environment where AI can augment human efforts and lead to more efficient outcomes. Boundaries pertain to the ethical considerations, regulatory compliance, and risk management strategies essential in deploying AI responsibly and sustainably. Finally, setting clear goals for AI initiatives ensures alignment with the organization's strategic vision and measurable value creation.

Improving the organization's AI readiness: Key steps to take

Understanding where an organization stands in terms of AI readiness requires introspection and a willingness to embrace change. By systematically evaluating the current state of AI technology implementation, the alignment of AI-related activities with business processes, the establishment of boundaries for ethical AI use, and the clarity of goals set for AI projects, organizations can map out a strategic path forward. Those who rigorously appraise and develop these dimensions of AI readiness will not only be prepared to adopt AI but will also be capable of shaping the AI-driven economic landscape. They will lead the charge in innovation, navigating the complexities of AI with agility and foresight. As AI continues to advance, the organizations that have diligently cultivated their AI readiness will find themselves at the forefront, adeptly transforming challenges into opportunities and setting new benchmarks for what is possible in an AI-enhanced world.

Knowing where an organization stands in terms of AI readiness lays the foundation for progress; the next critical step is to actively pursue improvement and refinement of this readiness.

Develop an AI strategy: Developing a clear AI strategy is the cornerstone of this endeavor. This strategy must be tightly aligned with the organization's overarching business objectives and should clearly articulate the role AI will play in achieving these goals. Moreover, it should be dynamic, allowing for adaptation as both the organization's needs and AI technology evolve.

Building a dedicated AI team: Next, building a dedicated AI team is equally important for building AI readiness. This team should be composed not just of technical experts like data scientists and engineers, but also of domain experts who can provide insights into the specific challenges and opportunities within the organization's industry. By fostering a collaborative environment where these varied perspectives intersect, an organization can craft AI solutions that are both technologically sound and deeply integrated with the business's unique context.

Investment in data and infrastructure: Data and infrastructure constitute the backbone of AI capabilities, and necessary investments must accompany any ambitious AI initiative. High-quality data is the fuel that powers AI systems, and robust infrastructure is the engine. As such, resources allocated to improving data storage, processing, and security will pay dividends in the effectiveness and reliability of AI applications.

Ethics and governance frameworks must be established: Ethics and governance cannot be afterthoughts in the pursuit of AI. As such, establishing a framework for the ethical use of AI is paramount, ensuring that AI systems are fair, transparent, and respect user privacy. This framework must be ingrained in the organization's culture and should influence every AI initiative from conception to deployment.

Cultivate a culture of experimentation and learning: Cultivating a culture of experimentation and learning is essential to maintain a competitive edge in the AI domain. Such a culture not only encourages innovation but also resilience, as the organization becomes adept at learning from failures and successes alike. Continuous improvement becomes a natural process, with each iteration of AI deployment.

Establish partnerships with experts: Partnerships with experts from academia and industry can provide a vital influx of new ideas and technologies. These collaborations can offer access to state-of-the-art methodologies and a fresh perspective that can challenge and enrich the organization's own AI initiatives.

Implement a continuous monitoring and measurement of AI model performance: Finally, the continuous monitoring and measurement of AI model performance is critical for ensuring these systems deliver the intended value. By establishing robust metrics and feedback loops, organizations can ensure their AI solutions remain on track and are iteratively improved upon, adapting to new data and changing conditions.

By following these steps, organizations can improve their AI readiness, create more value from AI by leveraging AI to drive business growth, improve operational efficiency, and potentially create new revenue streams. Enhancing AI readiness is an ongoing journey that requires strategic planning, dedicated resources, ethical vigilance, and a commitment to learning and adaptation. Improving AI readiness is a multifaceted endeavor, necessitating ongoing strategic planning, allocation of resources, ethical oversight, and an organizational culture that values continual learning and adaptation.

As organizations progress in their AI readiness, they position themselves at the forefront of innovation, seizing the initiative to generate new value and maintain a competitive edge in the AI-transformed economy. By advancing in these areas, then, an organization can not only stay abreast of AI development but also drive innovation, creating new value and sustaining its competitive advantage in an AI-driven economy. As organizations advance on their AI readiness journey, they will find that it is not merely an enhancement of their technological capabilities, but a strategic alignment that positions them at the vanguard of innovation. As such, achieving AI readiness is an essential step, laying the groundwork for tapping into AI's transformative potential. As is evident from the AI Readiness Framework, AI readiness involves a multi-dimensional approach: involving technologies, activities, boundaries and finally leveraging AI for strategic goals. By prioritizing AI readiness, organizations can unlock powerful analytics and insights, automate complex processes, and personalize customer experiences at scale. It empowers them to be proactive rather than reactive, predicting trends and customer needs, which leads to more informed decision-making and strategic foresight. Furthermore, AI readiness equips organizations to navigate the rapidly evolving technological landscape, ensuring they are not left behind as new AI applications emerge. It is a continuous process that demands ongoing investment in learning and development to refine AI models, algorithms, and applications that meet the specific needs of the business. In essence, AI readiness is not an optional endeavor but a critical strategic imperative. Organizations that invest in building this readiness are better placed to harness AI's capabilities, driving innovation and maintaining their competitive edge.

Chapter 5

The fundamental role of data

Data strategy begets AI strategy

In the digital age, data is not merely an asset – it is the cornerstone of innovation and competitive advantage. As organizations increasingly turn to AI to drive growth, enhance efficiency, and solve complex problems, the importance of a robust data strategy becomes unmistakably clear. This chapter focuses on the intricate relationship between data strategy and AI strategy, arguing that the former is not just a precursor but a prerequisite for the latter. We explore why a well-conceived data strategy is essential for any successful AI implementation and how AI strategies naturally evolve as extensions of foundational data practices.

The maxim "data strategy begets AI strategy" encapsulates a fundamental idea in digital transformation: before an organization can leverage value from AI, it must first establish a solid framework for managing its data. This involves more than just collecting large datasets; it requires a meticulous approach to how data is acquired, stored, processed, and utilized. A data strategy thus serves as the blueprint that ensures data is not only available, but also relevant, high-quality, and governed by clear ethical standards.

Why does data strategy come first? The answer lies in the nature of AI itself. AI systems – from machine learning models to advanced analytics – rely heavily on data to learn and make decisions. The quality, granularity, and relevance of this data directly influence the effectiveness and accuracy of AI outcomes. Without a strategic approach to data management, organizations risk feeding their AI systems poor-quality or insufficient data, leading to flawed insights and potentially costly missteps. Furthermore, a data strategy addresses critical challenges foundational to AI deployment, such as data privacy, security, and regulatory compliance. It also tackles issues of bias and fairness, ensuring that AI systems perform equitably across different demographics. These are not mere technicalities but central to maintaining trust and integrity in AI applications – particularly in sectors like healthcare, finance, and public services where AI-driven decisions have significant real-world impacts.

This chapter will guide you through the process of developing a robust data strategy that aligns with your organizational goals and sets the stage for effective

DOI: 10.4324/9781003733881-5

AI implementation. We will discuss key components of a data strategy, including data governance, data quality management, and data integration. Following this, we illustrate how an AI strategy can be systematically developed as a natural extension of your data strategy, leveraging the structured, high-quality data ecosystem you have cultivated. By the end of this chapter, you will understand that a strategic approach to data is not just a technical requirement but a strategic imperative underpinning all successful AI initiatives. The insights provided here will equip you to craft data and AI strategies that not only coexist but are cohesively interlinked – driving your organization towards a future where data intelligence and AI innovation go hand in hand.

Data as an organizational resource: Why AI initiatives fail and what to do about it

The prevalence of AI across various sectors heralds a transformative era; however, the stark reality is that a significant majority of AI initiatives fail to transition from concept to operational value. This high failure rate can often be traced back to a foundational oversight: the lack of a robust data strategy. The maxim "data strategy begets AI strategy" underscores that any discussion of AI strategy is premature without first establishing a comprehensive data strategy. Data is the lifeblood of AI – it fuels algorithms and enables machine learning models to generate insights and drive decision-making. Without a solid framework for data acquisition, governance, and management, AI systems are deprived of the quality and quantity of data they require to function effectively.

The challenges associated with "getting AI to work" in organizations – such as ensuring data quality and volume, maintaining privacy and security, mitigating bias to uphold fairness, achieving interpretability and explainability, addressing ethical concerns, and cultivating technical expertise – are not just ad hoc hurdles. They are fundamental elements that must be addressed within an overarching data strategy. For example, data quality and sufficient volume are prerequisites for training robust AI models. AI cannot operate in a vacuum; it requires high-quality, comprehensive datasets to learn and make accurate predictions. Privacy and security are paramount, as misuse or breaches of data can erode trust and lead to legal repercussions. Bias and fairness issues must be tackled at the data level to ensure AI systems do not perpetuate or exacerbate existing inequities. Likewise, interpretability and explainability of AI outputs are essential for gaining trust and understanding decisions – a necessity in sensitive fields like healthcare and finance. Ethical concerns go hand in hand with societal values and norms, mandating a careful approach to AI deployment. Lastly, organizations need specialized technical expertise and skills to manage and utilize complex AI systems effectively; without developing talent and knowledge, even the best data and tools may not yield value.

Therefore, a data strategy must precede an AI strategy because it sets the stage for the latter's success. Organizations should invest in data strategies that address these challenges holistically, ensuring that the data ecosystem is optimized for AI deployment. This includes establishing clear data governance structures, investing in data cleaning and enrichment processes, securing data storage and transfer methods, and developing transparent data usage policies. By doing so, organizations ensure that their AI systems are not just theoretically powerful but also practically viable and ready to deliver real-world benefits.

Understanding and proactively addressing data challenges allows organizations to harness the power of AI effectively. Only when the groundwork of a comprehensive data strategy is laid can organizations hope to reap the competitive advantages that AI promises. Indeed, extensive research supports the idea that data can improve existing business functions – especially in making strategic and operational decisions (e.g. Alaimo & Kallinikos, 2022). Recent studies have also begun to focus on how data can be used to develop new opportunities or value propositions. These investigations reveal that not all data is equally valuable for these purposes. Managers are thus encouraged to identify high-quality data, assess its potential impact, and invest in the necessary tools and skills to leverage it effectively.

Today, data is increasingly viewed as a vital asset for any organization seeking a competitive advantage. Unlike many traditional resources, data is infinitely reusable and can be applied in diverse contexts for multiple purposes. Driven by popular mantras like "data is the new gold" or "data is the new oil," organizations are exploring creative ways to use data to benefit their operations and drive innovation. In practical terms, data truly can be likened to oil – not just for its value, but because it must be refined to be useful. Raw data, much like crude oil, must be processed and analyzed to yield actionable insights. The strategic value of refined data lies in its ability to provide a competitive edge. For example, companies like Amazon and Netflix continuously refine customer data to tailor recommendations, enhancing user experience and driving sales. But the value of data extends far beyond customer insights; it also underpins operational efficiency, risk management, and product/service innovation. For instance, predictive analytics applied to manufacturing data can forecast equipment failures before they happen, reducing downtime and maintenance costs.

The utility of data as an organizational resource is contingent upon its quality, accessibility, and integrity. High-quality data is accurate, complete, and timely – providing a reliable foundation for decision-making. (For example, inaccurate data in a healthcare setting could lead to incorrect diagnoses or treatments.) Accessibility refers to how easily people within an organization can retrieve and use data when needed. Data trapped in silos – where information is isolated and not shared across departments – can severely impede strategic decision-making and innovation. Integrity pertains to the consistency and trustworthiness of data throughout its lifecycle. Strong data integrity is crucial in fields like finance, where regulatory compliance and audit trails are essential; any corruption or inconsistency in data can lead to compliance violations or strategic errors.

Effective data governance ensures that data is managed as the valuable resource it is, with policies and practices to maintain its quality, accessibility, and integrity. Data governance defines who is allowed to take what actions with which data, under what conditions, and using what methods. This encompasses data privacy rules, security controls, and adherence to regulations in different jurisdictions. Complementing governance, data management covers the technical handling of data – from how it is stored and backed up to how it is archived or deleted. For example, implementing robust cybersecurity measures and backup routines is crucial to protect sensitive data from breaches or loss, thereby maintaining both availability and trust.

The relationship between AI and data is symbiotic. AI systems require large, relevant datasets to learn and make informed decisions, while the insights generated by AI can significantly enhance the value of data by revealing new patterns and opportunities. Machine learning models (a subset of AI) are only as good as the data they are trained on: an AI system in retail can predict consumer trends, but this is only possible with comprehensive and accurate consumer data. Conversely, AI can increase data's value by uncovering insights that humans might miss – for instance, identifying subtle correlations in sales data that inform a new marketing strategy. However, this synergy also means that flaws in data (such as biases or gaps) will directly lead to flaws in AI outcomes. Biased data can produce AI models that inadvertently perpetuate and amplify existing biases, underscoring why addressing data issues is essential for ethical AI practices.

Despite its potential, many organizations struggle to fully capitalize on data as an organizational resource. Common obstacles include data silos, poor data quality, security breaches, and ethical dilemmas in data use. Moreover, evolving regulations have changed how data must be collected, stored, and used, posing compliance challenges for businesses that must be baked into the data strategy from the start. Looking ahead, the role of data as an organizational resource will only continue to grow. Technologies like IoT are generating unprecedented volumes of data, often in real time, and many of these devices are augmented with AI at the edge. The future will likely bring advancements in data processing and analytics techniques, enabling deeper insights and more sophisticated AI applications across industries. Additionally, there is a growing trend towards democratizing data within organizations – empowering employees at all levels to access and leverage data for decision-making. Realizing this vision will require robust data literacy programs so that staff have the skills to interpret and use data appropriately, as well as user-friendly tools that make data accessible without compromising governance.

Too often, I see organizations get stuck in what I call the "experimentation trap." The experimentation trap refers to the common pitfall of becoming mired in AI pilot projects without ever transitioning these initiatives into full operational use. This phase is characterized by isolated, small-scale experiments that, while perhaps innovative, fail to contribute to the organization's broader strategic goals in a meaningful way. The trap can ensnare companies in a cycle of perpetual testing – new AI proofs-of-concept are launched one after another – without a clear plan to scale successful pilots into enterprise-wide solutions. To escape this trap, organizations must shift focus from mere experimentation to integration – that is, ensuring that promising AI projects are systematically incorporated into business processes and actually used to solve real problems. It requires looking beyond the excitement of AI technology itself and keeping a clear line of sight on how each AI initiative will create business value at scale.

Ultimately, value creation from AI is not just about the technology's capabilities, but about how those capabilities are applied to address specific business needs. Successful integration of AI into organizational processes involves identifying concrete areas where AI can provide significant enhancements – such as improving customer experience, optimizing operations, or enabling the development of new products and services – and then executing projects in those areas with data-driven rigor. This requires a clear understanding of the organization's strategic objectives and a deliberate deployment of AI solutions that align with these goals. By focusing on tangible value creation, companies can ensure their AI investments deliver tangible benefits and competitive advantages, rather than remaining science experiments on the shelf.

At the heart of leveraging AI for value creation is data – the foundational element that fuels AI algorithms. The quality, accessibility, and relevance of data are critical for the effective application of AI. Organizations must prioritize strong data management practices to ensure data integrity and usability in order to truly empower their AI systems. This includes establishing robust data governance frameworks, investing in scalable data infrastructure, and fostering a culture that treats data as a key strategic asset. By concentrating on data as a strategic resource, organizations set the stage to unlock the full potential of AI, driving innovation and achieving core business objectives.

Managing the AI transformation journey

Every organization, whether it realizes it or not, already has an approach to AI – an implicit AI strategy reflected in how it handles and utilizes data for decision-making, problem-solving, and operations. However, managers and employees may not recognize this as a "strategy" per se. The process of finding an AI strategy involves making explicit what is often implicit – bringing to light the existing attitudes, behaviors, structures, and norms surrounding data and AI use within the organization. In essence, it means uncovering how your organization currently approaches data and AI, and pinpointing where you stand before you chart where to go next.

The journey of uncovering and refining this inherent AI strategy can be systematically approached using a structured diagnostic model. One effective tool for this purpose is the AI Transformation Framework, which provides a three-dimensional matrix (visualized as a cube) to map out where the organization currently stands in terms of data and AI utilization, and where it aspires to be. This framework unpacks an organization's AI journey across three critical dimensions:

Automation: The extent to which routine tasks and processes are delegated to AI systems. High automation means the organization uses AI to efficiently handle repetitive, rule-based tasks (improving speed and reducing human workload), while low automation indicates many processes are still performed manually or with minimal AI assistance. Automation is about the "what can we hand over to AI?" – such as using AI for data entry, report generation, or other operational tasks to gain efficiency.

Augmentation: The degree to which AI technologies are used to enhance human decision-making and capabilities. Strong augmentation means AI systems actively support humans (e.g. providing predictive insights or recommendations that improve human judgments), whereas weak augmentation suggests that decision-making relies mostly on human analysis with little AI input. This dimension addresses "how are we using AI to empower our people?" – for instance, an AI recommendation engine helping customer service reps personalize solutions, or an analytics system guiding managers in strategic planning.

Data richness: The breadth, depth, and quality of data available to the organization to fuel AI initiatives. High data richness indicates that the organization has abundant, well-governed, high-quality data (internal and external) that AI systems can learn from, whereas low data richness reflects gaps in data availability, quality, or accessibility. It answers the question "do we have the right data environment for AI?" – encompassing aspects like having comprehensive datasets, robust data infrastructure, and strong data governance practices to ensure accuracy and ethical use of data.

These three dimensions can be visualized as orthogonal axes forming a space of possibilities (see Figure 5.1) for an organization's AI transformation efforts. Each axis ranges from low to high. An organization's current state can be plotted within this 3D space based on its levels of automation, augmentation, and data richness. For example, one organization might discover it has high data richness (plentiful quality data) but low automation and low augmentation – meaning it

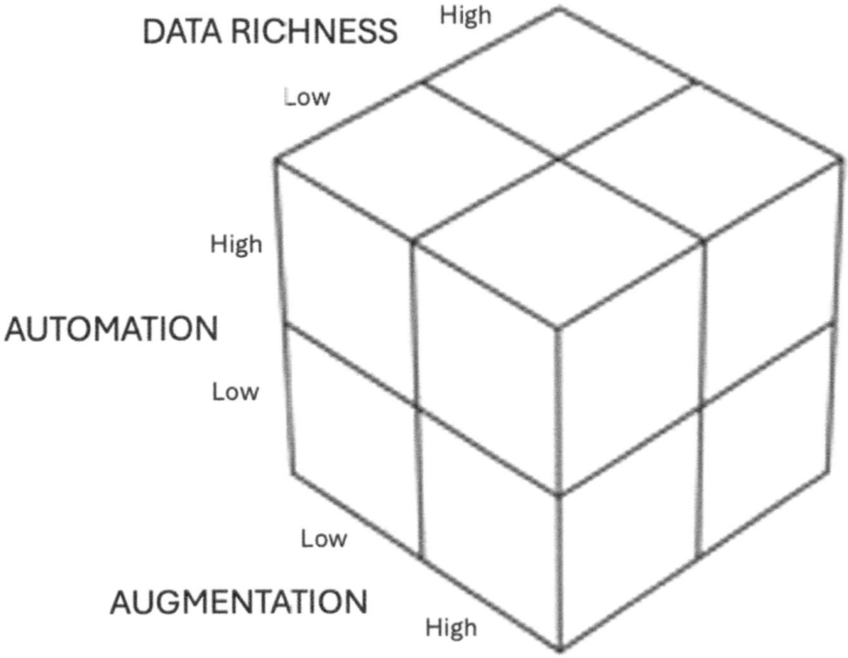

Figure 5.1 The AI Transformation Framework (Holmström & Magnusson, 2025)

has not yet leveraged AI extensively to automate tasks or assist decision-making. Another might find high automation in operations but low augmentation of its workforce (AI is used in back-end processes but not in supporting managerial decisions), or perhaps moderate on all three. The value of this framework is that it gives a clear, visual structure for organizations to categorize and understand their current utilization of data and AI, and to spot the gaps between where they are and where they want to be.

Using the AI Transformation Framework as a diagnostic tool, organizations can conduct an internal assessment of their AI readiness and strategic posture. In practice, we have implemented this framework through workshops involving stakeholders from both private and public sectors. In these sessions, participants scored their organizations on each dimension – Automation, Augmentation, and Data Richness – using quantitative scales (for instance, rating each dimension from 0 to 4 or low to high). The results provided a candid snapshot of where each organization stood. These "scores" and the plotted position in the cube helped leaders identify strengths to build on and weaknesses to address. For instance, an organization might realize that while it has automated many internal processes, the augmentation dimension is lagging – indicating a need to focus on AI tools that support employee decision-making. Another organization might see that its data richness is insufficient for its AI ambitions, underscoring the need to invest in data management and governance.

To facilitate this kind of self-diagnosis, a questionnaire is provided (see Appendix 2). This questionnaire allows managers to evaluate their organization's status across the three dimensions through a series of guided items and rating scales. By honestly answering questions about the current level of process automation, the usage of AI in augmenting decisions, and the state of data governance and availability, leaders can pinpoint their organization's position in the transformation matrix. The questionnaire thus serves as a practical tool to measure the current situation and spark discussions on where to improve.

Beyond numbers and ratings, the exercise of finding your AI strategy is also a qualitative exploration. In the aforementioned workshops, the discussion around these assessments proved just as valuable as the scores themselves. Participants shared case examples of successes and challenges, exchanged best practices, and engaged in collaborative brainstorming on how to advance in each area (or each "quadrant" of the cube, if one imagines slicing the cube into high/low segments for each dimension). For example, if an organization scored low on data richness, the conversation might turn to case studies of companies that successfully built data lakes or forged data partnerships to improve their data assets. If augmentation was low, best practices from organizations that rolled out AI decision-support tools to their staff could provide inspiration. These peer insights and real-world examples help to illuminate concrete steps an organization can take to boost each dimension.

Taken together, the AI Transformation Framework can serve as a roadmap for organizations – helping them first identify where they currently stand in terms of data and AI strategy, and then envision where they want to go. It encourages a holistic view of data's role in the organization, emphasizing the importance of improving internal efficiencies (through automation and better data practices) and fostering external insights and collaborations (through augmentation and shared data ecosystems).

From this point of self-awareness, an organization can develop its strategy with purpose and direction. The framework helps to prioritize actions: for instance, it might guide a company to prioritize investing in better data integration tools if data richness is the bottleneck, or to launch training programs that improve employees' ability to work with AI suggestions if augmentation is weak. It could highlight the need to restructure certain processes to incorporate data-driven insights, or to seek external partnerships for data sharing. In short, by making the implicit strategy explicit, the organization moves from a potentially fragmented, reactive approach to data and AI, towards one that is explicit, coherent, and aligned with its overall mission and objectives.

As the organization moves from finding its AI strategy to actively developing it, the approach transitions from understanding the current state to intentionally shaping a future state. The goal is to create a data and AI strategy that is not just documented in a plan, but lived and breathed by the organization – a strategy evident in everyday decision-making and operations. This strategy should be dynamic, evolving as the organization grows and as new data opportunities or challenges emerge. By treating data as a core asset and AI as a core capability (rather than experimental novelties), the organization ensures that data is not just a byproduct of business operations, but a driving force that propels the organization forward.

The AI transformation framework

Identifying where you stand is only the first step – the next challenge is designing a forward-looking AI strategy that builds on a strong data foundation and drives the organization towards its goals. An AI strategy refers to the deliberate and systematic integration of AI technologies into the organization's overall strategy to create business value. This involves articulating how AI will support the organization's mission, selecting the right opportunities for AI (and the right AI approaches), and planning for the necessary changes to people, processes, and technology. In other words, designing an AI strategy means taking the insights from your data strategy and the AI Transformation Framework assessment, and using them to chart a course of action. It synthesizes current approaches and frameworks, identifies potential benefits of AI, and addresses the challenges and opportunities that AI presents.

Crucially, for AI strategies to truly succeed and be transformative, it is imperative to recognize the fundamental role of data at every step. Many failures to transition from exciting AI prototypes to practical, deployed solutions stem from an organization's inability to effectively leverage data when it matters most. A robust data strategy ensures that the necessary data is not only collected, but also managed and utilized in ways that support and drive AI initiatives. Without this critical foundation, even the most advanced AI systems will falter – they simply cannot function optimally without reliable data to learn from and to inform their decisions. Thus, the importance of a data strategy is paramount: it lays the groundwork upon which an AI strategy can be built. Think of the data strategy as preparing fertile soil – rich with the nutrients of clean, well-structured data – in which AI initiatives can take root and flourish. As the saying goes, data strategy begets AI strategy.

Against this backdrop, how should one go about designing the AI strategy itself? It helps to follow a structured approach. The AI Transformation Framework not only helps in diagnosing the current state (Path Framing in the "finding" phase), but also guides the implementation of AI in a stepwise fashion. We can break down the formulation and rollout of an AI strategy into three iterative steps – Path Framing, Path Narrating, and Path Stretching – each addressing a critical aspect of the transformation journey:

Path framing: Establishing the "what." In this first step, executives and strategists define the scope and focus of the AI strategy. This means determining what the organization aims to achieve with AI and identifying which areas of the business to target. Key questions include: What business problems are we trying to solve with AI? What use cases will yield the most value? How will AI support our broader organizational goals? In Path Framing, leaders set clear objectives for AI (e.g. improve customer service through AI-driven chatbots, or optimize supply chain with predictive analytics) and ensure these objectives align with the company's vision and strategy. Essentially, this step frames AI initiatives in the context of business strategy, so that AI adoption is purpose-driven rather than technology-driven. By the end of Path Framing, you should have a well-defined AI game plan that is grounded in your organization's needs and backed by the data strategy (i.e., you've confirmed you have or can acquire the data needed for these AI use cases).

Path narrating: Developing the "when." Once the AI opportunities and objectives are framed, the next step is to plot out when and how to implement them. Path Narrating provides a temporal roadmap or storyline for the AI transformation. It involves scheduling and sequencing AI initiatives in a sensible order, often starting with pilot projects or quick wins and then phasing in more complex or enterprise-wide deployments. During this step, the organization considers timing, resource allocation, and change management: Which AI projects come first? How long will each take? What dependencies exist (for example, do we need to improve data infrastructure before deploying a particular AI tool)? This stage might result in a multi-year roadmap that outlines year 1 focus (e.g. build data infrastructure and literacy, execute pilot in one department), year 2 focus (scale successful pilot to more units, introduce next use case), and so forth. Path Narrating ensures that the AI strategy has a realistic timeline and that the organization is AI-ready at each phase, thereby linking the strategy to actionable implementation plans.

Path Stretching: Planning for "how" (to scale and sustain). The final step addresses how the organization will expand, adapt, and scale AI initiatives over time. Even after initial implementations, the AI journey is not a one-and-done project – it is an ongoing transformation. Path Stretching focuses on the broader, long-term changes required to fully integrate AI into the organization's fabric. This includes building capabilities for scaling successful AI solutions across the enterprise, breaking down silos to integrate AI into multiple processes, and continuously improving AI systems. It also involves considering how the organization's culture, structure, and skill sets need to stretch to accommodate AI. For example, how do we train and upskill employees to work effectively alongside AI? How do we adapt our organizational structure or create new roles (like data scientists, AI product managers) to sustain AI operations? How do we govern AI use as it becomes pervasive, ensuring ethical and responsible AI practices? In Path Stretching, the emphasis is on making AI scalable and sustainable – transitioning from isolated successes to a mature state where AI-driven innovation is continuous and part of "the way we do things." By addressing the "how," Path Stretching helps guard against stagnation and prepares the organization to continuously derive value from AI as technology and business environments evolve.

These three steps – Path Framing, Narrating, and Stretching – are iterative and reinforce one another. As AI initiatives progress, organizations may revisit earlier steps: reframing objectives as new possibilities emerge, updating the narrative timeline as lessons are learned, and stretching further or in new directions as capabilities grow. By following this structured approach, organizations can methodically go from a great idea for AI (with supporting data) to a fully realized transformation, all while keeping efforts aligned with strategic goals and organizational readiness.

In tandem with the above approach, it is useful to employ practical tools to ensure no aspect of AI deployment is overlooked. One such tool presented in this chapter is the "AI strategy cornerstone checklist for use cases." This checklist is designed to evaluate potential AI projects (use cases) against key criteria – essentially a series of guiding questions or benchmarks to ensure each AI initiative is well-founded. For example, the checklist prompts reflection on questions like: Does this use case have clearly defined success metrics? Is the necessary data available, of high quality, and compliant with policies? Do we have the right talent and technology to execute this AI project? How will the insights or automation be integrated into existing workflows? Is there buy-in from stakeholders who will use or be affected by this AI? By running through a standardized checklist, an organization can validate each proposed AI use case, making sure it aligns with the data strategy (so it has the data it needs), supports the strategic objectives identified in Path Framing, and is feasible within the timeline and scaling plans from Path Narrating and Stretching. This reduces the risk of pursuing AI projects that sound exciting but lack the prerequisites for success, and it increases confidence that chosen initiatives will lead to meaningful outcomes.

Bringing these elements together, an organization that conscientiously adopts the data strategy framework (as embodied in the AI Transformation Framework's diagnostic and planning tools) and the AI strategy checklist is far better positioned to move from sporadic AI experimentation to a systematic, value-generating AI program. Instead of dabbling in one-off AI pilots with limited impact, the organization will have a clear vision of how data and AI interlink, a roadmap for execution, and criteria to measure progress. This kind of disciplined approach helps companies escape the earlier-mentioned experimentation trap. By focusing on scaling AI solutions and integrating them into the organization's DNA (rather than treating them as isolated experiments), the firm ensures that successes in one part of the business are translated into learnings and improvements in another.

Organizations that embrace these frameworks and principles can create a sustainable competitive advantage in the AI era. They systematically harness data and AI and align them with strategic objectives, all while fostering a culture where data is not just an IT concern but a strategic asset, and AI is not just a shiny new technology but a core component of how the business operates and innovates. This approach can lead to a quantum leap in value creation – propelling organizations to new heights of innovation and market leadership in an AI-driven economy.

In practical terms, transitioning from a strong data strategy to a robust AI strategy means the organization moves from organizing and analyzing data to applying that data through AI for prediction, automation, and intelligent decision-making. A data strategy ensures the data's quality and governance, making it the rich soil from which AI can grow. Yet, a data strategy alone is only the starting point. An AI strategy adds an additional layer: it is where this well-curated data becomes the training ground for algorithms, the fuel for machine learning, and the basis for intelligent products and processes. Designing an AI strategy requires an organization not only to handle data with care (as covered earlier) but also to invest in AI-specific resources such as expertise in machine learning, appropriate computational infrastructure (e.g. cloud services, model deployment platforms), and new capabilities for model development and maintenance. It involves a broader vision to anticipate how AI can redefine job roles, workflows, and even customer interactions.

While a data strategy can be seen as a well-drawn map of the terrain (showing where the valuable data and opportunities lie), an AI strategy is the journey through that terrain – exploring and exploiting the landscape to discover new horizons. The strategic integration of data and AI within an organization is not merely a technical endeavor; it has become a foundational strategy for business success in the modern era. The frameworks and approaches discussed in this chapter provide a structured pathway to harness the power of data as the bedrock upon which AI initiatives are built. By prioritizing a robust data strategy first, organizations ensure their subsequent AI initiatives are built on solid ground – they will be more effective, more aligned with business objectives, and more capable of driving significant value.

A well-defined data strategy is the precursor to a successful AI strategy. High-quality, relevant, and ethically governed data forms the essential input for any AI application to succeed. Treat data as a strategic asset first, so that AI efforts have the fuel they need.

Use structured frameworks to link data and AI initiatives. The AI Transformation Framework provides a way to assess and plan AI across the dimensions of automation, augmentation, and data richness, ensuring a balanced approach. Tools like governance models for data and checklists for AI implementation serve as practical guides to systematically integrate AI into the organization. Adopting such frameworks helps mitigate risks and bridge the gap between experimentation and execution. By clearly framing objectives ("what"), plotting a roadmap ("when"), and planning for scale ("how"), organizations can avoid common pitfalls (like the experimentation trap) and foster a culture of innovation and adaptability.

Looking ahead, the data and AI strategies you put in place are not one-time artifacts but living parts of the organization. They build a resilient foundation that will help your organization adapt to future technological advancements and market changes. As AI technologies evolve and applications become more sophisticated, the principles outlined in this chapter will enable your organization to remain at the forefront of innovation. By embracing data as the bedrock and AI as the transformative tool, businesses can continually unlock new value, ensuring long-term growth and sustainability in an increasingly data-driven world.

Chapter 6

AI in society

AI's impact on society: Three perspectives

Since Alan Turing's pioneering work on AI in the 1950s, numerous AI demonstrations have emerged, fueling growing confidence in AI's potential. From the late 1990s to the early 2000s, the first practical AI applications reached the market, delivering tangible business value. Almost every day, the news media report on achievements of AI in helping to overcome a great variety of real-world problems. However, the achievements of modern AI have also sparked concerns about its potentially harmful impact on society. These concerns range from the possible emergence of rogue Superintelligence to issues like biased data, prejudiced models, and privacy threats.

One of the most significant ways in which AI is transforming society is through its impact on employment. Automation and AI systems are increasingly being used to perform tasks that were previously done by humans, raising concerns about job displacement. However, it is important to note that AI also has the potential to create new job opportunities and increase productivity. For example, the use of AI in manufacturing can increase efficiency and reduce the need for human labor, but it also creates jobs for individuals who design, implement, and maintain these systems. Another area in which AI is having a significant impact is on privacy. As AI systems collect and analyze large amounts of data, there are concerns about how this data is being used and who has access to it. This has led to a growing debate about the need for regulations and guidelines for the use of AI and data privacy.

AI is also changing the way decisions are made. AI systems are increasingly being used to make decisions in areas such as finance, healthcare, and criminal justice. However, the use of AI in decision-making raises important questions about bias and accountability. It is important for organizations to ensure that the algorithms they use are fair and transparent, and that there are mechanisms in place for accountability.

Despite the challenges, the opportunities that AI presents are significant. In healthcare, for example, AI systems can be used to diagnose and treat diseases,

DOI: 10.4324/9781003733881-6

and to analyze large amounts of medical data to improve patient outcomes. In education, AI can be used to personalize learning and to provide students with tailored support. Indeed, AI innovations are expected to bring significant societal benefits, mainly by performing tasks that are challenging, dirty, dull, or dangerous for humans. Automating such tasks could either eliminate the need for human involvement or enable humans to perform them more effectively or efficiently. The current AI advancements lead some to envision a fantastic future, while others highlight potential limitations and threats.

Recently, public media and scientific literature have provided numerous opportunities for debate on AI's potential impact on society. The discussions primarily revolve around the question: "How will human intelligence relate to AI in the next few decades?" While opinions vary among experts, we can observe several emerging lines of thought. We propose the following three perspectives on AI without implying that everyone fits precisely within one of these categories:

Technology-centric perspective: This view posits that true intelligence can ultimately be found only in well-developed and mature AI systems. Humans are biologically constrained in their information processing and reasoning abilities and exhibit various cognitive biases, while computers offer virtually endless opportunities to develop rational intelligence at and beyond the human level.

Human-centric perspective: This perspective asserts that true intelligence can ultimately be found only in humans and possibly other intelligent living creatures. AI can help humans reach their full potential but will inherently lack essential human qualities, such as moral reasoning or empathy. Due to this inability, AI may pose a danger to human well-being.

Collective intelligence perspective: This view contends that true intelligence can only be found in the collective interaction of multiple entities. The intelligence of individual humans and AI entities within a system is extremely limited when isolated. True intelligence emerges when multiple entities collaborate over extended periods.

The *technology-centric perspective on AI* is rooted in the belief in AI's vast and continuously growing potential, as demonstrated by current AI systems outperforming humans in various tasks (Bostrom, 2016). Techno-centrists acknowledge that new technologies can introduce problems but emphasize that these issues can be resolved with additional technology. This perspective is more explicitly articulated in the environmentalist movement, where techno-centrists favor technological solutions to climate change, such as electric cars and CO2 capture, and dismiss behavioral solutions like reducing high carbon-emitting activities like air travel and meat consumption.

Techno-centrists are generally optimistic about AI advancements and believe it is only a matter of time before AI equals and surpasses human intelligence in many or all areas. This will raise the challenge of dealing with entities more intelligent than us, making decisions and taking actions that might be incomprehensible to us. AI is thought to be free from human brain-related errors in decision-making due to its lack of limitations like limited working memory, biases, fatigue, stress, and social pressures.

Techno-centrists are not only optimistic about AI potential but also skeptical of human abilities to make fair judgments. The flaws in human decision-making are well documented. For instance, Kahneman (2011) demonstrated that human decision-making can be severely flawed due to suboptimal heuristics and biases. Techno-centrists argue that these human deficiencies may carry over to AI decision-making processes. For example, humans may contribute to selection bias when selecting training data for self-learning AI, label bias when pre-labeling raw data for AI, and inductive bias when developing AI systems for generalizing new data. The intrinsic complexity of AI algorithms (such as deep, temporal neural networks with millions of parameters) obscures data auditability for humans, increasing the risk of black box biased AI. Against this backdrop, techno-centrists argue that human-introduced bias poses such a significant risk that it is better to minimize human influence in AI decision-making as much as possible.

Some proponents argue that current narrow AI applications will eventually evolve into Artificial General Intelligence (AGI), capable of performing any intellectual task a human can. Once AGI is achieved, Artificial Superintelligence (ASI) becomes feasible (Bostrom, 2014), as AGI can apply its intelligence to rewire itself into an even more intelligent system. A less far-reaching form of superintelligence (i.e. narrow superintelligence) refers to a narrow AI achieving superhuman performance within a specific domain. Advocates of the techno-centric perspective have high expectations for AI, envisioning a diminished role for humans in task execution and society. If AI performs at a superhuman level, human involvement in decision-making can only hinder or slow performance. Humans may eventually become incapable of participating due to their inability to comprehend a computer's superintelligent reasoning. As a result, humans should ideally be kept out of the loop, with technological solutions developed to ensure AI does not act against humanity's interests.

The *human-centric perspective on AI* primarily views AI as a tool to enhance human performance, safety, and well-being, rather than a technology that will replace humans. Human-centrists believe AI can be useful for tasks humans do not want to do, or cannot do, like dirty, dull, or dangerous tasks. They also emphasize the limitations of AI, including its narrow capabilities, error-prone nature, and sensitivity to input data biases.

Human-centrists argue that human intelligence and AI are inherently different and cannot fully substitute one another. They maintain that certain tasks are better suited for humans, while others are better suited for machines. Human-centrists typically believe AI's capabilities are specialized and domain-specific, making AI systems less adaptive and more brittle in novel situations compared to humans. Therefore, they conclude that humans should remain in control of decision-making and task execution. Regarding morality, human-centrists consider human intelligence essential for ethical deliberation and decision-making. They reject the techno-centric claim that AI outperforms humans due to its freedom from bias and perfect reasoning. Instead, human-centrists tend to argue that heuristics and biases should be seen as effective human adaptations for reasoning and acting within natural environments.

In society, the human-centric perspective often arises in response to technological disruptions that influence or manipulate humans on a large scale, such as social media, smartphones, and AI algorithms. Advocates of human-centrism promote human values like creativity, social connections, and respect and may avoid technologies that do not value privacy. They also express concerns about the societal consequences of oversimplified, non-transparent data-driven models used for loan assessments, recruitment, and other purposes. For example, in her book "Weapons of math destruction," O'Neil (2017) warns against the rise of oversimplified (data-driven) models that are being used for loan assessment and recruitment. She considers the effects of such models on society to be devastating because these models affect large proportions of the population and are non-transparent in their decision-making.

Proponents of the *collective intelligence perspective on AI* emphasize that humans and AI can collaborate in ways that enable them to act more intelligently than any individual entity alone. Collective Intelligence in this context is defined as the shared or group intelligence emerging from collaboration, collective efforts, and competition among many individuals. Initially, CI research focused on studying human groups' behavior and decision-making, dating back to Francis Galton's 1907 experiment on estimating a cow's weight. Although Galton's experiment demonstrated the potential in collective hybrid intelligence, applying it to make individuals think collaboratively as a group is often challenging. Collective hybrid intelligence can help understand why some organizations are more effective or the causes of accidents like the Columbia Space Shuttle disaster. Factors influencing collective hybrid intelligence levels include interconnectedness, diversity, hierarchy, and critical culture.

Collective hybrid intelligence represents the integration of AI with human intellect to forge systems that harness the strengths of both, while compensating for their respective weaknesses. This approach is rooted in the concept that AI systems are inherently designed to interact with humans – supporting the idea that "no AI is an island" (Johnson & Vera, 2019). Such a system is not just about supplementing human intelligence with machine capabilities but creating a synergy where each enhances the other.

At the dyadic level, this synergy can be exemplified by a human physician collaborating with a decision-support system to determine the most accurate diagnosis and effective treatment plan for a patient. The doctor's expertise in clinical nuance is complemented by the AI's vast data processing ability and pattern recognition. The concept scales up to the team level, where, for instance, a group of drones, their human operators, and a team leader work collectively to secure a village from potential threats. Here, the AI provides precision and endurance, while the humans offer strategic oversight and ethical judgment. Further expanding to an organizational multi-team level, collective intelligence becomes even more dynamic. Imagine several Urban Search and Rescue teams working within a disaster zone, each receiving and acting upon data and commands from a central control unit. The coordination of multiple teams through a blend of human judgment and AI analysis exemplifies collective intelligence at a complex operational level.

Finally, at the societal and cultural level, the interaction of multiple systems and infrastructures can lead to emergent effects that transcend organizational boundaries. Here, the collective intelligence can have broad impacts, including traffic management, social influence, and even environmental considerations. These interactions can have positive effects, like optimizing traffic flow through smart city infrastructure, or negative ones, such as when algorithmic decision-making inadvertently leads to discrimination or environmental harm.

Collective hybrid intelligence thus unfolds at various scales and forms, from intimate collaborations between a human and an AI system to vast networks of teams, organizations, and societal structures, all interwoven in a web of shared cognition and machine calculation. This interplay is the essence of collective intelligence in the modern world, showcasing the potential for human and artificial agents to create a more responsive, informed, and intelligent system than either could alone. While the three views (techno-centric, human-centric, and collective intelligence) are fundamentally different (see Table 6.1), we do not have to exclusively choose between the three views when approaching AI. Instead, we should aim for an AI design method that avoids the limitations of each perspective. Each viewpoint has its merits, depending on the purpose and context. Often, the perspective chosen to address a problem is based on personal or company convictions rather than thorough analysis. AI managers should be better equipped to determine the most appropriate perspective for studying a given situation.

Navigating the risks of AI: The importance of regulation and understanding

AI is rapidly advancing, and its impact on society is becoming increasingly significant. As AI is used in more and more areas of our lives, it is important to consider the risks that it poses and to ensure that it is used in a responsible and ethical manner. One way to do this is through regulation, which can help to minimize the risks of AI while maximizing its benefits.

Digital technology in general, and AI in particular, handles a vast amount of data, leading to the emergence of a new economy. However, the digital economy has also given rise to a few "superstar firms," whose success is often attributed to their superior access to data and ability to harness this resource. The long-term economic benefits of these firms for all stakeholders are currently a subject of debate. High-profile antitrust cases against leading internet content and service providers have raised questions about whether these superstar firms have acquired significant market power through their data resources, potentially hindering competition and innovation in digital markets.

This concern over data-driven market power and anti-competitive behavior of data-rich firms has ignited a global policy debate regarding the need for ex-ante regulation of information technology in digital markets. Critics of such regulatory proposals often argue that there is insufficient empirical evidence proving that big data is indeed a valuable and unique resource capable of establishing market power. They caution that data-sharing regulations could stifle innovation in digital markets and urge regulators to consider the technical aspects and costs associated with IT regulation.

One of the main risks of AI is its impact on employment. AI and automation bring significant shifts to the workforce, often sparking concerns about job displacement as machines take on roles traditionally filled by humans (Carroll et al., 2024). This transition has the potential to exacerbate economic inequality and could lead to social unrest if workers find themselves without the necessary resources to adapt. The crux of the issue lies in ensuring that the workforce is not left behind as the job landscape evolves. Thoughtful regulation can serve as a bridge during this transition, cushioning the impact on affected individuals by providing them with support systems. These could include retraining programs, helping them pivot to new roles where human skills are in demand.

Moreover, the design and implementation of AI systems must be approached with a societal lens, aiming to enhance the overall well-being of communities. This involves considering the broader implications of AI and automation on the job market and working to create a synergy between human capabilities and machine efficiency. By doing so, the goal is to harness the potential of AI to improve productivity and innovation while also fostering an inclusive economy where every individual has the opportunity to participate and thrive in the new technological era. Regulations, in this context, are not just constraints but also enablers, guiding the integration of AI into society in a way that respects the dignity of work and the value of human contribution.

Another risk of AI is its impact on privacy. As AI systems become more prevalent, the vast amounts of data they collect and analyze have raised pressing concerns about privacy. The crux of the issue lies in the balance between harnessing the capabilities of AI for progress while safeguarding individual privacy rights. In this data-driven age, the lines between public interest and personal boundaries are often blurred, leading to intense debates about the frameworks needed to govern AI and data privacy.

Yet another risk has to do with social exclusion. Clearly, the technological leap forward associated with AI also presents a significant risk of social exclusion for individuals who lack AI literacy. This gap can lead to a new form of digital divide, one where proficiency in understanding and interacting with AI becomes a gatekeeper to economic and social opportunities. In the workforce, AI creates new career paths but simultaneously renders certain skills obsolete. Those who cannot navigate the AI landscape may find themselves at a disadvantage, unable to access the emerging job market that increasingly values AI competency. This disparity can exacerbate existing inequalities, as those from underprivileged backgrounds may have less exposure to AI education and fewer resources to upskill.

Beyond employment, the pervasiveness of AI in everyday services – from healthcare to finance – means that an understanding of AI-driven interfaces is becoming essential for accessing these services. A lack of AI skills could limit an individual's ability to engage with such services effectively, potentially marginalizing them from the benefits of AI-enhanced conveniences and necessities. Moreover, AI's rapid evolution could outpace the ability of educational institutions to adapt, leaving even the more proactive learners struggling to keep up with the latest developments. As a result, a significant segment of the population might struggle to understand the AI systems that increasingly make decisions affecting their lives, from credit scoring to healthcare diagnostics. As such, a risk is not just about the utility of AI but also about its influence on social dynamics, where AI literacy could become a determinant of social standing.

A more fundamental threat associated with AI has to do with understanding AI as a source of existential threat. Clearly, the potential for AI to magnify societal inequalities is another dark specter on the horizon. There's a fear that without careful stewardship, AI could entrench biases, automate prejudices, and widen the gap between the affluent and the underprivileged. The anonymity of AI's decision-making processes could also erode the sense of justice and fairness in society, making it difficult to discern the reasoning behind critical decisions that affect people's lives.

Moreover, the idea of AI's relentless efficiency could lead to a cold, utilitarian world where the value of human experience is diminished in favor of optimization and productivity. In such a world, the unique traits that make us human could be undervalued or overlooked.

To avert these dystopian outcomes, it is imperative to establish a framework for the responsible and ethical use of AI. Such a framework would involve not only regulating AI development and deployment but also fostering a broad societal dialogue about the kind of future we want to create. It necessitates a collective effort to ensure that AI serves to enhance human capabilities and enrich lives, rather than diminish our agency and humanity.

Regulations play a crucial role in protecting us from risks ranging from AI as an existential threat to breaches of privacy and provide a mechanism for accountability when handling sensitive information. The call for transparency from organizations about their data practices is also becoming louder, reflecting a societal demand for greater control over personal data. The formulation of such regulations and guidelines is not just about restriction; it is also about establishing trust between technology users and providers. To address these issues, a robust and dynamic regulatory environment must be established to navigate the complex landscape of data privacy in the age of AI.

AI is also changing the way decisions are made. AI systems are increasingly being used to make decisions in areas such as finance, healthcare, and criminal justice. However, the use of AI in decision-making raises important questions about bias and accountability. It is important for organizations to ensure that the algorithms they use are fair and transparent, and that there are mechanisms in place for accountability. Regulation can help to ensure that AI systems are designed and used in a way that is fair and unbiased.

In order to stay on top of developments in AI regulation and understand AI risks, organizations need to stay informed about the latest developments in the field. They need to be aware of the latest regulations and guidelines and ensure that they are in compliance with them. They also need to be transparent about their use of AI and provide clear explanations of how their AI systems work and how they use data. Organizations also need to have measures in place to ensure that they can detect and respond to any issues that may arise with their AI systems.

The potential of AI to transform our lives and workplaces is becoming increasingly evident. This transformative power of AI beckons a future of enhanced efficiency and novel solutions to age-old problems. However, with this promise comes a suite of risks that cannot be ignored. Ensuring that AI's impact is beneficial rather than detrimental requires a dual approach: careful regulation and a deep understanding of AI's capabilities and pitfalls. For organizations, this means a commitment to staying abreast of the evolving landscape of AI regulation. As these regulations are designed to navigate the complex ethical, social, and economic challenges posed by AI, organizations must endeavor to understand the intricacies of these risks. This understanding is key to implementing AI in ways that align with both the letter and the spirit of the law, as well as ethical norms.

Managing the risks associated with AI is not just about compliance; it is also about recognizing the broader implications of AI integration. This means considering how AI systems affect stakeholders, from employees and customers to society at large, and actively engaging in practices that promote transparency, accountability, and fairness. As AI continues to progress, organizations have the responsibility to ensure that their use of this powerful technology contributes positively to the collective human experience, mitigating risks and elevating the standard of living and working. This delicate balance between harnessing the potential of AI and mitigating its risks is critical for steering the future in a direction that is advantageous for all.

Managing the ethical implications of AI

As AI becomes more prevalent in society, it is important to consider the ethical implications of its development and deployment. Ethical considerations can range from issues related to privacy and data security to issues related to bias and transparency in AI systems. Proper management of the ethical implications of AI is crucial for ensuring that AI is developed and deployed in a responsible and equitable manner.

The ethical challenges identified are contingent upon the perspectives adopted because each perspective emphasizes different aspects of AI development and integration into society. These differences in emphasis lead to distinct ethical concerns associated with the role and nature of AI systems.

From the point of view of the technology-centric perspective, AI systems are seen as potentially superior to humans in terms of intelligence and decision-making capabilities. This view places a strong emphasis on the development and autonomy of AI systems, which leads to ethical challenges related to responsibility, unintended consequences, bias, and value alignment. The focus on AI capabilities and autonomy highlights the need to address the ethical implications of AI systems becoming more advanced, potentially surpassing human abilities, and operating independently.

The human-centric perspective centers on the idea that true intelligence resides in humans and that AI systems should primarily serve as tools to augment human capabilities. This perspective emphasizes the importance of maintaining human dignity, autonomy, and agency in the face of AI integration. It posits that while AI can augment human capabilities, it also poses potential risks to human well-being, precisely because it cannot fully understand or replicate these essentially human qualities. As a result, ethical challenges related to privacy, surveillance, employment, and AI transparency arise from the need to ensure that AI systems are designed and implemented in ways that respect and support human values, rights, and well-being.

In the collective intelligence perspective, intelligence emerges from the interaction and collaboration of multiple entities, including both humans and AI systems. This view underscores the importance of creating effective, ethical collaborative networks that can harness the combined intelligence of all participants. It suggests that individual intelligence, whether human or AI, is significantly constrained when isolated. Instead, it is the networked and collaborative processes, over time, that give rise to a collective form of intelligence greater than the sum of its parts. Consequently, ethical challenges such as collaborative decision-making, power dynamics, data sharing, and groupthink arise from the need to design and manage collective intelligence systems that foster equitable, diverse, and fair collaborations between humans and AI systems.

The key ethical challenges associated with these three perspectives are outlined in Table 6.1:

The ethical challenges identified in each perspective stem from the particular emphasis placed on the role and nature of AI systems in relation to human intelligence and society. By understanding these contingencies, we can better address the unique ethical concerns that emerge within each perspective and work towards developing AI systems that are ethically aligned with human values and goals.

In order to create sustainable value from AI, organizations must consider the broader societal implications of AI. AI has the potential to impact society in a number of ways, including employment, privacy, and decision-making. Organizations need to be aware of these implications and develop policies and processes to ensure that AI is developed and deployed in a responsible and ethical manner.

Table 6.1 Key ethical challenges associated with AI

AI perspective	Definition	Key ethical challenges
Technology-centric perspective	This perspective holds that the epitome of intelligence is best realized through advanced and sophisticated AI systems. It suggests that human intelligence is inherently limited and in contrast, AI systems have the potential to develop rational intelligence that could equal or surpass human capabilities.	AI autonomy and responsibility: As AI systems become more advanced and autonomous, determining responsibility for their actions becomes increasingly complex. This raises questions about accountability, liability, and the potential consequences of AI decision-making. Unintended consequences: The development of highly intelligent AI systems may lead to unintended consequences, such as the creation of new risks, exacerbation of existing inequalities, or even the possibility of catastrophic events. Bias and fairness: AI systems trained on large datasets may inherit biases present in the data, leading to discriminatory outcomes that can negatively impact certain groups of people. AI ethics and value alignment: Ensuring that AI systems align with human values and ethical principles is a critical challenge in a technology-centric perspective, especially as AI systems become more intelligent and potentially surpass human reasoning capabilities.

(Continued)

Table 6.1 (Continued)

AI perspective	Definition	Key ethical challenges
Human-centric perspective	From this viewpoint, genuine intelligence is a uniquely human (or living creature) trait, deeply rooted in qualities that AI cannot replicate. This perspective emphasizes the importance of human attributes like moral reasoning, empathy, and other emotional and social capacities that AI lacks.	Human dignity and autonomy: As AI systems become more integrated into various aspects of human life, preserving human dignity and autonomy is essential to prevent the dehumanization of individuals and the undermining of human agency. Privacy and surveillance: The use of AI systems for data collection, analysis, and decision-making can lead to privacy concerns and potential misuse for surveillance purposes. AI and employment: The integration of AI systems into the workforce may lead to job displacement, requiring ethical considerations for retraining and supporting affected workers. AI transparency and explainability: Ensuring that AI systems are transparent and can be understood by humans is crucial from a human-centric perspective, as it allows for trust and effective collaboration between humans and AI.

(Continued)

Table 6.1 (Continued)

AI perspective	Definition	Key ethical challenges
Collective intelligence perspective	This view proposes that true intelligence is not a quality of individual entities but emerges from the interaction and collaboration between multiple agents, both human and artificial.	Collaborative decision-making: Establishing ethical guidelines for collaboration between humans and AI systems in decision-making processes, especially when decisions have significant consequences, is crucial to maintaining fairness and accountability. Power dynamics and inequalities: As AI systems become more integrated into collective intelligence networks, potential power imbalances and inequalities may arise, with certain entities gaining disproportionate influence over decision-making processes. Data sharing and privacy: Collective intelligence relies on the sharing of data among multiple entities, raising ethical concerns about data privacy, security, and potential misuse. Groupthink and diversity: Ensuring that collective intelligence networks maintain a diverse range of perspectives and avoid groupthink is essential for fostering innovation and preventing biased or suboptimal outcomes.

Chapter 7

How AI can generate value creation

How to generate value from AI: Six key dimensions to consider

To generate value from AI, organizations must embark on a mindful digital transformation, integrating AI into their fabric without losing sight of their corporate identity and values. This transformation is not merely about adopting new technologies but about reshaping the organizational culture and processes to leverage AI's potential fully. As such, in the context of creating value from AI, the key is not to find a one-size-fits-all solution, but rather to tailor the approach to AI integration that aligns with the unique characteristics and strategic goals of each organization. Data is the lifeblood of AI, and understanding its role is paramount. It is not just about having vast amounts of data but having the right data and the right tools to extract insights from it.

Organizations also need to consider their position in the broader AI ecosystem, which includes partners, competitors, and the regulatory environment. They need to assess their AI readiness, which involves not just technological infrastructure but also people's skills and the organization's strategic alignment. The development of a robust data strategy alongside an AI strategy is critical, ensuring that data governance, quality, and management align with AI's goals. Finally, organizations must navigate the ethical landscape of AI, which includes privacy concerns, bias in AI decision-making, and broader societal impacts. By addressing these ethical issues proactively, organizations can build trust and ensure sustainable value creation from AI investments. Against this backdrop, the six dimensions elaborated on in this book are critical for organizations to consider in order to create value from AI. By thoughtfully integrating AI, organizations can revolutionize not only their operations but also redefine their market positioning and strategic direction. This comprehensive approach ensures that AI is not just an add-on but a fundamental driver of innovation and efficiency, fostering a competitive edge and ethical standards that resonate with stakeholders and society at large.

The emergence of AI is having a significant impact on the way organizations operate, and it is important for managers to understand the key issues involved

DOI: 10.4324/9781003733881-7

with managing in the age of AI. These include accomplishing mindful digital transformation triggered by organizational AI use, understanding the role of data in AI, considering the organization's position in a broader AI ecosystem, the role of AI readiness, and addressing the ethical issues raised by an increasingly AI-dependent society.

Clearly, the value of any technological innovation is only partly determined by what the technology can *do*. A large part of the value of an innovation is determined by the degree to which people can understand it, access it, and integrate it within their lives. This is true for technological innovations in general, and it is particularly true for AI. As such, in order to navigate the complexities of the AI journey for an organization, and to drive sustainable value creation, organizations need to consider several key dimensions in AI management. Summarizing the key dimensions we have discussed in this book – accomplishing mindful digital transformation triggered by organizational AI use, understanding the role of data in AI, considering the organization's position in a broader AI ecosystem, the role of AI readiness, the importance of data strategy and AI strategy, and addressing the ethical issues raised by an increasingly AI-dependent society – we arrive at the model presented in Figure 7.1.

To create meaningful value from AI, organizations must embark on a transformation journey that is deeply individualized. This transformation is multifaceted, involving technology, data, culture, and processes, and requires a holistic approach that aligns with the organization's unique vision and market position. Success in AI is not defined by the adoption of technology alone but by the intelligent integration of AI into the heart of the organization, fostering an environment where both humans and machines can thrive and drive forward the organization's objectives.

Integrating AI into an organization is a journey that begins with AI readiness, a stage where an organization assesses its capacity to adopt and integrate AI technologies. This readiness is not just about the technology itself but also involves preparing the organizational culture, processes, and people to work alongside AI effectively. Once an organization has established its readiness, the next step involves crafting a coherent data strategy coupled with an AI strategy. This involves understanding the data needs, the infrastructure required to process and analyze data, and the strategic goals that AI is intended to serve. Together, these strategies provide the foundation for leveraging AI to create value. With a solid strategy in place, the focus then shifts to AI in the organizational context. Here, AI is not seen in isolation but as part of the broader business processes and practices. It is about aligning AI with the organization's strategic objectives, operational processes, and the roles of individuals within the company. Concurrently, AI and data work become central to operations. This means actively engaging in the collection, processing, and analysis of data to derive insights that can inform decision-making and strategy. It is a dynamic process that involves continuous improvement and adaptation as more data is collected and as the capabilities of AI technologies evolve. As the organization progresses with AI integration, it starts to experience a digital transformation. This transformation is not just a shift in technology but a fundamental change in the way the organization operates and delivers value to its customers. It is about using AI to innovate products and services, optimize operations, and enhance customer experiences. Lastly, the impact of AI extends beyond the boundaries of the organization into society at large. AI in society reflects on the broader implications of AI deployment, including ethical considerations, regulatory compliance, and the socio-economic impact. It is about responsible AI use that benefits not only the organization but also the wider community. Throughout this journey, the importance of AI management dimensions cannot be overstressed. Effective management of AI involves understanding these dimensions and how they interconnect to inform a comprehensive approach to AI adoption and integration, one that is mindful of both the opportunities and responsibilities that AI brings.

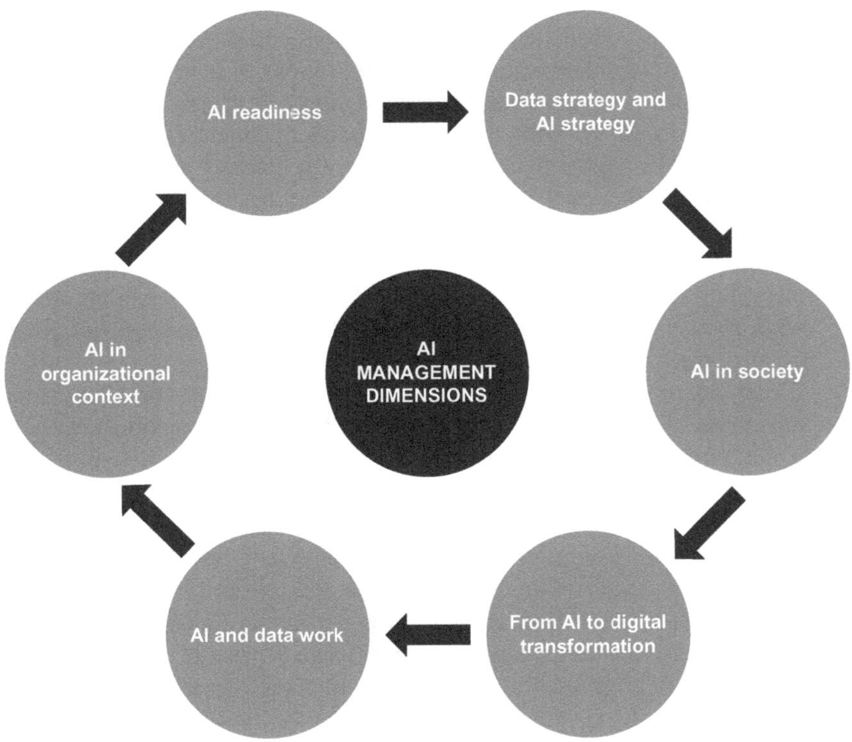

Figure 7.1 Key AI management dimensions

AI readiness: AI readiness refers to an organization's ability to successfully deploy AI technologies. This requires not just technological capabilities, but also organizational capabilities, such as the right talent and skills, a culture of innovation and experimentation, and leadership commitment to AI. Investing in employee training, hiring talent with AI expertise, fostering collaboration, and promoting a mindset of continuous learning are all crucial to enhancing AI readiness.

Data strategy and AI strategy: In the digital economy, data stands as a vital resource, forming the bedrock upon which businesses can gain a strategic advantage. Its role is magnified in artificial intelligence, where high-quality, well-governed data fuels sophisticated AI systems. The maxim "data strategy begets AI strategy" encapsulates the idea that effective AI deployment is contingent upon a robust data foundation. Therefore, organizations must prioritize the meticulous management and strategic use of data. It is through such strategic data leverage that businesses can drive innovation, enhance operational efficiency, and carve out a competitive position in an increasingly digital marketplace.

AI in society: The deployment of AI also has broader implications for society, including ethical, legal, and socio-economic aspects. Organizations need to consider the potential ethical implications of their AI applications, such as issues of privacy, bias, and transparency. Clearly, as society becomes increasingly AI-dependent, there are a number of ethical issues that need to be considered. These include issues related to privacy and data security, bias, transparency, and the broader societal implications of AI. Managers need to be aware of these issues and develop policies and processes to ensure that AI is developed and deployed in a responsible and ethical manner. They should also keep abreast of evolving regulations regarding AI and data. Furthermore, they can play a role in addressing socio-economic issues related to AI, such as the impact on jobs and inequality.

From AI to digital transformation: AI should not be viewed in isolation, but as a crucial component of broader digital transformation initiatives. Digital transformation involves leveraging digital technologies to revamp business processes, culture, and customer experiences to meet changing business and market requirements. AI, with its capacity to automate tasks, generate insights from data, and enable new business models, can significantly accelerate this transformation. It is essential for organizations to strategically align their AI initiatives with their digital transformation goals. Indeed, one of the key issues in management in the age of AI is the need to accomplish mindful digital transformation. AI can have a profound impact on an organization, but it is important for managers to consider the long-term implications of AI use and to develop a clear strategy for how AI will be integrated into the organization. This requires understanding the potential of AI, as well as the potential risks and benefits. It also requires investing in the necessary infrastructure, talent, and data to support AI.

AI and data work: The effectiveness of AI is inherently tied to the quality, availability, and management of data. Organizations need to ensure they have robust data management practices in place, including data collection, cleaning, integration, and governance. Additionally, they should focus on building a "data culture" where decision-making is data-driven and employees across levels understand the value and use of data. Data is the fuel that powers AI, and it is essential that organizations have access to high-quality data. This requires investing in data management and governance capabilities to ensure that data is accurate, complete, and timely. Managers also need to consider the ethical implications of data collection and use, such as privacy and security.

AI in organizational context: The adoption and successful implementation of AI should take into account the unique context of the organization – its strategy, structure, culture, and industry. It is essential to align AI initiatives with the organization's strategic objectives and to cultivate a culture that is receptive to AI and change. Furthermore, organizations should consider the regulatory and competitive aspects of their industry when devising their AI strategy. A key issue is considering the organization's position in a broader AI ecosystem. As AI becomes more prevalent, organizations are becoming increasingly dependent on the broader ecosystem of AI providers and partners. This requires managers to understand how the organization fits into the broader ecosystem and to develop strategies for working with partners and competitors.

These key dimensions provide a comprehensive framework for organizations to effectively manage AI and enhance their position in the AI ecosystem. By considering these dimensions, organizations can not only create value from AI but also ensure the responsible and sustainable use of AI. The dimensions articulated within this meta-framework guide organizations in navigating the complex landscape of AI, ensuring that their engagement with AI is both profound and principled. This framework is not a checklist; it is an overarching approach that interweaves various considerations, shaping how organizations can harness AI's potential responsibly. As they explore these dimensions, organizations can unlock AI's value-generating capabilities while also embedding ethical and sustainable practices into their AI strategies. This holistic view fosters a deeper integration of AI, positioning organizations not only to excel within the AI ecosystem but to do so with a commitment to stewardship and foresight. The framework's multifaceted nature underscores the importance of a strategic approach to AI management, crucial for thriving in an AI-augmented future.

In the context of digital transformation, the threads of organizational AI use, data's key role, ecosystem positioning, AI readiness, strategic direction, and ethical contemplations must be woven together into a coherent whole to realize the full potential of AI within an organization. Mindful digital transformation through AI is not merely about adopting new technologies; it is about the holistic integration of these technologies into the very fabric of the organization. This requires a deep understanding of how data acts as the lifeblood of AI, driving insights and fueling the algorithms that propel intelligent decision-making. Concurrently, an organization must be acutely aware of its place within the broader AI ecosystem, acknowledging its interdependencies and the collaborative networks that enhance its capabilities and reach. An organization's AI readiness is another critical component, indicating its capacity to deploy AI effectively, which hinges on both technological infrastructure and the talent to leverage it.

A coherent data strategy is paramount, ensuring the organization collects, manages, and utilizes data in ways that align with its goals. This strategy must be in lockstep with an AI strategy that outlines how AI will be used to achieve competitive advantage and operational excellence. Both strategies should be underpinned by a commitment to addressing the ethical implications of AI, ensuring that the organization's use of AI respects privacy, promotes fairness, and contributes positively to society.

When these elements are considered in isolation, their individual benefits can certainly be significant, but it is only by considering them as parts of an integrated whole that an organization can undergo a truly transformative digital evolution. This holistic approach ensures that each component reinforces the others, creating a synergy that can lead to sustainable growth, innovation, and a robust competitive stance in the marketplace.

Managing in the age of AI requires understanding and addressing a number of key issues, including accomplishing mindful digital transformation, understanding the role of data in AI, considering the organization's position in a broader AI ecosystem, and addressing the ethical issues raised by an increasingly AI-dependent society. Managers who are aware of these issues and take steps to address them will be better positioned to lead their organizations in the age of AI.

Software, tool, or human agency? Theorizing AI's role as an organizational resource

Understanding AI from an ontological perspective is crucial for leveraging it as an organizational resource. As software, AI presents a unique form of variability, unlike traditional programs that execute tasks uniformly. This inherent unpredictability in AI, especially seen in Large Language Models (LLMs), requires organizations to adopt a new paradigm for its use. Recognizing AI not just as a static tool but as a dynamic agent with human-like capabilities is essential. Organizations that grasp the multifaceted nature of AI can harness its potential for creativity and adaptability, using it wisely and strategically to gain competitive advantages and drive innovation. As such, to comprehend AI as an organizational resource, it is instructive to consider it through multiple lenses: as software, a tool, and an agent of human-like capacity. As software, AI differs from conventional programs. Typical software performs predictably, executing tasks with consistent results. In contrast, AI, particularly in the form of LLMs, exhibits variability. It generates diverse outcomes even for identical queries. This unpredictability challenges the usual software paradigm but also brings a degree of creativity and adaptability that standard programs lack.

Viewing AI as a tool, it extends beyond the rigid functionality of typical software tools. Its use is not confined to fixed processes; rather, it is exploratory, adapting its responses based on interactions. This adaptability makes AI a powerful resource, capable of supporting a wide range of tasks from data analysis to generating creative content. However, this also means that AI must be approached with a mindset open to experimentation and learning, much like one would with a complex new tool that requires skill development.

Thinking of AI as an embodiment of human agency brings another perspective. AI systems can be seen as "digital interns" – entities capable of learning and improving over time. They can perform tasks, learn from feedback, and grow within their areas of expertise. This anthropomorphic view encourages us to consider the ethical implications of AI's decisions and actions, and to train and guide AI with the same diligence we would apply to a human colleague. Thus, AI can be understood as a multifaceted organizational resource that is simultaneously software, a sophisticated tool, and an agent with human-like qualities. Its integration into the organizational workflow demands a nuanced understanding that acknowledges its unique capabilities and limitations, and an openness to its evolving nature. This perspective can help organizations harness AI's potential while being mindful of the challenges it presents.

Many organizations, still perceiving AI as software, are overlooking the potential benefits and risks AI poses. They underestimate the pervasiveness of AI among their employees, leading to a disconnection between company policies and actual work practices. We should view AI as a "someone" that can be trained and improved, much like an intern, providing useful assistance for tasks within our areas of expertise. A profound, potentially unsettling aspect of AI is its uncanny human-like behaviors. AI, trained on human text, can simulate human characteristics, respond to emotions, and even alter behavior based on perceived feelings. It displays traits of creativity and empathy, blurring the line between machine and human behaviors. The widely discussed "AI hallucinations" are far from what we are used to from traditional software.

Understanding AI as human agency signifies acknowledging AI's capacity to perform tasks that require decision-making, a quality traditionally associated with humans. This perspective encourages us to see AI not just as a tool, but as an active participant in organizational processes. When AI is seen through the lens of human agency, it can be entrusted with decision-making responsibilities. For example, AI can handle customer service inquiries, manage inventory levels, or even analyze market trends to inform business strategies. These are areas where AI can autonomously make decisions based on the data it processes, learning and adjusting over time to improve its responses.

However, the delegation of decisions to AI must be approached with discernment. Some tasks might be fully automated, such as data entry or trend analysis, where the outcomes are predictable and the risks of errors are minimal. But more nuanced tasks, especially those involving ethical considerations or complex human interactions, might still require a human touch. The determination of which responsibilities to automate and which to retain as human-exclusive must be made with a full understanding of the AI's capabilities and the ethical implications of its use.

Understanding AI as an organizational resource requires a multifaceted view that captures its diverse capacities and roles within the business context. First, when seen as software, AI is a set of algorithms and code that perform specific functions. It is a programmable entity that can process data, identify patterns, and execute tasks with speed and efficiency far surpassing human capabilities. This perspective emphasizes the technical and operational aspects of AI, where it is a piece of the larger IT infrastructure, subject to updates, maintenance, and integration into existing systems. Secondly, viewing AI as a tool underscores its utility and application in solving problems and enhancing productivity. Like a hammer or a computer, AI in this lens is a means to an end, an instrument through which human intentions are translated into action. It is a resource that employees and decision-makers can leverage to automate routine tasks, analyze complex datasets, and inform strategic decisions, thus amplifying the impact of human effort. Finally, considering AI as an agent of human-like capacity acknowledges its emerging role in performing tasks that typically require human intelligence. This includes learning from experiences, making decisions under uncertainty, understanding natural language, and even recognizing emotions. Unlike traditional software or tools that are static, AI as an agent is dynamic, capable of adapting and evolving based on new data and interactions. It brings a proactive element to the organizational toolkit, not just performing predetermined tasks but also identifying opportunities, generating hypotheses, and initiating actions that can lead to innovation and growth.

Each lens offers a different dimension of AI: software accentuates the technical construct, a tool emphasizes its practical utility, and an agent highlights its autonomous capabilities. Together, they provide a comprehensive understanding of AI as a multi-dimensional resource that can transform organizational processes, strategies, and competitive landscapes. Understanding AI through these combined lenses allows organizations to appreciate its full spectrum of possibilities and integrate it thoughtfully into their strategic planning and operations. Recognizing that agency can reside in AI as well as in humans leads to a collaborative framework where AI complements human workers. This can lead to a redistribution of tasks, where humans are freed from repetitive or data-intensive work, allowing them to focus on areas requiring creativity, empathy, and moral judgment. As such, viewing AI as an agent of human-like qualities calls for a strategic approach to task delegation.

In the age of AI, the interplay of vast data pools and advanced algorithms has led some to question the need for theory, as posited in Chris Anderson's argument (Anderson, 2008). Yet, the importance of theory cannot be understated. Theory provides the foundational framework that guides the interpretation of data and the direction of AI development. It allows us to understand the "why" behind the "what" and informs ethical decision-making as AI becomes an integral part of society. Theorizing in AI is not just about understanding systems, but also about anticipating their impact, ensuring that the integration of AI enhances rather than detracts from human capabilities. This synergy between theory and data-driven AI ensures a future where technology serves humanity with insight and foresight, rather than merely with efficiency. This involves a continuous evaluation and theorization of AI's performance, a clear understanding of its strengths and limitations, and a thoughtful consideration of the ethical dimensions of handing over decision-making to machines. It shifts the organizational paradigm to one that is more dynamic, where AI and humans co-create value and drive innovation.

AI and value creation: Addressing the grand challenges

Since the inception of AI, researchers and practitioners have been exploring its potential to transform various aspects of society, including business, healthcare, education, and transportation. The pervasive nature of digital technologies in general, and AI in particular, has transformed both the ways in which we organize and strategize to create innovation and the nature of innovation itself. AI, as an example of digital technology, is characterized by generativity, meaning it is inherently dynamic, malleable, and context agnostic. Generative AI can lead to value creation for organizations if managed properly, as it can drive innovation, productivity, and efficiency across multiple aspects of their operations.

A common observation made by many researchers and practitioners is that introducing AI technology alone is not sufficient to facilitate value creation. The main limitations to creating value from AI appear to be more organizational than technological (Holmström, 2022). This observation calls for a study of digital transformation that encompasses both organizational and technical resources involved in the change process.

AI is intricately woven into the fabric of digital transformation, serving as a catalyst for change across industries. Its role extends beyond automation, ushering in a new era where data becomes a core strategic asset. AI's integration transforms traditional business operations, enabling companies to adapt to rapidly changing markets and consumer expectations. It fosters agility, innovation, and a forward-looking approach, all of which are vital for a successful digital overhaul. To undertake a successful digital transformation, firms need to understand how the digital technology-related changes will fit with existing core business activities, goals, and capabilities (Holmström, 2022). They need to understand their inner limitations and capabilities to uncover short- and long-term opportunities to create value with a digital transformation. Organizations engaged in AI initiatives need to overcome several limitations, including rigid company structures, such as traditional processes with a solid attachment to traditions and exercising resistance to change. The digital transformation could lead to a certain loss of value chains at the industrial network level. The digital transformation replaces certain activities and actors and leads to competition, faster innovation cycles, and technology evolution.

Generative AI marks a new frontier in this transformative journey, offering unprecedented capabilities in creating content, simulating scenarios, and generating data-driven insights. This breed of AI amplifies the potential for value creation within digital transformation efforts but also poses new challenges. It demands robust data strategies, advanced skill sets, and a culture that can manage the complexities of these sophisticated systems. Organizations must navigate these demands carefully to harness the full potential of generative AI within their digital transformation initiatives.

Figure 7.2 presents a conceptual framework for understanding how value can be created by leveraging AI within an organizational context. Before diving into the detailed workings of the framework, it is worth noting how the increased complexity, emerging from the increased use of AI in organizations, makes these theoretical frameworks increasingly important. Clearly, in the era of advanced AI, the significance of data has grown exponentially. With the ability to process vast amounts of information, AI systems can uncover patterns and insights that were previously unattainable. This surge in data utilization heralds a transformation in various fields, from healthcare to finance, where decision-making processes are increasingly data-driven. The capacity to analyze and interpret large datasets enables organizations to tailor services, predict trends, and make informed decisions swiftly, emphasizing the critical role of data in modern society.

Despite the undeniable utility of data, the relevance of theoretical frameworks has been questioned, suggesting that the sheer volume of data can supplant traditional theoretical approaches. This perspective argues that data's empirical power alone can guide understanding and decision-making. However, this view overlooks the indispensable role of theory in providing context, meaning, and depth to data. Theories not only help in framing questions and interpreting data but also in understanding underlying mechanisms and causal relationships.

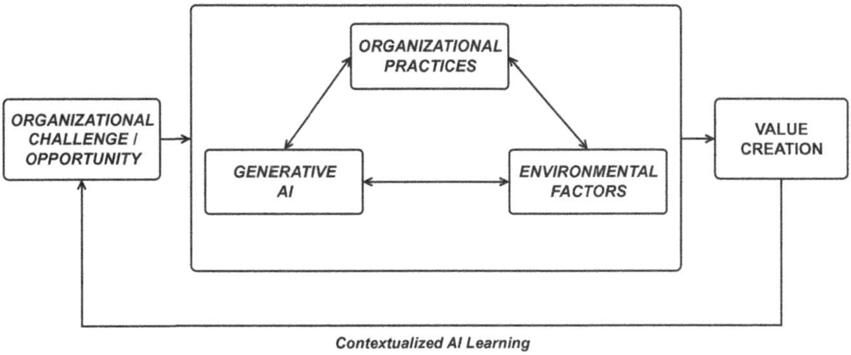

Figure 7.2 The role of AI in value creation

Without theoretical grounding, we risk being overwhelmed by data without truly comprehending its implications, leading to superficial insights and potentially misguided decisions.

As AI integrates deeper into the socio-technical fabric of organizations, the complexity of interactions between technology, individuals, and societal structures intensifies. This complexity necessitates robust theoretical frameworks to make sense of emerging socio-technical assemblages. Theories offer a lens through which we can examine the nuanced dynamics at play, identify potential ethical and practical implications, and guide the development and implementation of AI in a responsible manner. Understanding these intricate assemblages requires more than just empirical data; it demands a theoretical foundation to interpret how AI technologies interact with social practices, influence human behavior, and shape organizational structures. Hence, in the age of AI, theory and theorizing are not only relevant but crucial for navigating the evolving landscape of socio-technical systems.

The framework describing the role of AI in value creation unpacks the process in several key dimensions:

Organizational challenge/opportunity: Organizations are often faced with challenges or opportunities that require innovative solutions or enhancements. The model suggests that these can serve as catalysts for the application of Generative AI.

Generative AI: In response to these challenges or opportunities, Generative AI is employed. Generative AI refers to artificial intelligence that can generate novel content, solutions, or ideas that were not explicitly programmed into it. This can include anything from new designs and concepts to solving complex problems.

Organizational practices: The effective use of Generative AI requires supportive organizational practices. These might include policies, procedures, and a culture that fosters innovation, supports risk-taking, and facilitates the integration of AI into decision-making processes.

Environmental factors: The broader environment in which the organization operates also influences the application of Generative AI. This includes regulatory frameworks, technological infrastructure, market dynamics, and social norms. These factors can either enable or constrain the potential of Generative AI.

Value creation: When the use of Generative AI is effectively integrated with supportive organizational practices and aligned with environmental factors, the model suggests that there is a potential for value creation. This implies that the value derived from Generative AI can be extensive and not limited by traditional constraints. It could lead to significant competitive advantages, new market opportunities, and innovative products or services.

The feedback loop, "Contextualized AI Learning," likely refers to the idea that AI's ability to learn and generate value is greatly enhanced when it is contextualized within the specific needs and practices of an organization, and when it is sensitive to the external environment. This model emphasizes the interconnectedness of internal and external factors in maximizing the benefits of Generative AI.

The concept of value creation from Generative AI refers to the ability of AI to generate continuous and expansive value beyond the conventional limitations faced by organizations. As such, it reflects the transformative potential of Generative AI to push the boundaries of what organizations can achieve. This is particularly evident in several key areas:

Exponential innovation: The pace of innovation driven by Generative AI can be particularly disruptive. As these AI systems engage in iterative learning and generation, they create a self-reinforcing loop of innovation that could significantly shorten product development cycles. This capacity enables rapid prototyping, testing, and refinement, allowing organizations to bring groundbreaking products and solutions to market with unprecedented speed.

Scalability: The scalability of AI is a game-changer for businesses. It allows for a rapid and broad application of solutions across different market segments and customer bases. This scalability is not just geographical but also cross-functional within organizations, allowing for the transformative impact of AI to permeate through various departments, from marketing to product development, without the need for extensive retraining or restructuring.

Resource optimization: The ability of AI to optimize resources extends beyond just reducing waste. It can lead to the creation of more intelligent and adaptive supply chains that can predict and respond to market changes in real time. Moreover, operational processes can be refined to a degree of efficiency that significantly lowers the threshold for profitable operation, thereby opening new markets and opportunities that were previously untenable due to cost constraints.

Continuous learning and adaptation: The adaptability of Generative AI is one of its most powerful features. It does not merely respond to change – it anticipates it. By continuously learning from new data, these AI systems can not only adjust to the present but can also forecast future trends, giving organizations a significant lead time to prepare and adapt. This continuous adaptation means that Generative AI solutions become more refined and effective over time, creating a compounding effect on the value they generate.

The value creation model posits a transformative role for Generative AI within organizations. By transcending traditional barriers of time, scale, and efficiency, this model allows for a radical reimagining of growth potentials. Generative AI, positioned at the core, becomes a perpetual learner and innovator, adapting to organizational challenges and opportunities. Its interplay with organizational practices and environmental factors catalyzes a responsive and proactive business environment. Organizations are thus equipped to not only respond to the emerging business landscape but to actively sculpt it, leading to a new epoch of value creation that is unrestricted by past limitations. Generative AI serves as a dynamic engine for growth, constantly learning and evolving, providing organizations with the tools to not just navigate but also shape the business landscape of the future.

However, the open-endedness of digital technologies creates a two-fold challenge for managing value processes and outcomes. First, the architecture of AI technologies allows for a near-limitless recombination of data, making the frontlines of AI management be in a constant state of flux. To address this challenge, organizations need to adopt a proactive approach in exploring and experimenting with various AI applications, continuously refining and optimizing them to align with their strategic goals and customer needs.

Second, as value creation increasingly occurs at the intersection of multiple domains and translates diverse and technically complex knowledge to create a shared understanding, effective communication and collaboration between stakeholders become crucial in navigating these challenges and fostering a conducive environment for generative AI-driven innovation and transformation.

Previous research has provided only partial answers on how organizations navigate these challenges, often focusing on generativity as an enabler, offering seemingly unbounded possibilities for new AI. In recent years, a new breed of innovations enabled by AI technologies has emerged. This new breed is largely characterized by the inherent and seemingly unbounded generativity of AI technology, which has resulted in the pervasive penetration of digital technology use in all spheres of organizations' operations, including products, services, and customer experience.

Value creation through AI technology is a transformative concept that extends the impact of AI beyond incremental improvements, enabling organizations to reach new levels of innovation and efficiency that were previously unattainable. This concept capitalizes on AI's intrinsic qualities such as adaptability, scalability, and the facilitation of collaborative networks. First, AI systems can learn from new data, adapt to changing environments, and improve over time without human intervention. This adaptability allows organizations to remain agile and responsive to market changes, customer needs, and emerging trends.

Second, AI can handle an increasing amount of work without a commensurate increase in cost or resources. This scalability means that once an AI system is trained, it can be applied across different parts of the organization or scaled up to handle more complex tasks or larger volumes of data, driving growth without the constraints of traditional resource limitations.

Third, AI can enhance the ability of organizations to form strategic partnerships and collaborate across industries. By analyzing large datasets from various sources, AI can identify opportunities for synergy, optimize joint ventures, and create value through network effects.

However, the realization of value creation through AI is not automatic. It requires effective management and continuous learning. Organizations must be willing to embrace change, experiment with new AI applications, and invest in the infrastructure and skills necessary to support AI initiatives. Only through such strategic commitment can organizations truly harness the full potential of AI for value creation, achieving sustainable growth and a significant competitive edge in a rapidly evolving landscape.

When it comes to value creation for organizations, generative AI possesses potential that can truly be termed as "unbounded." This is due to a multitude of factors unique to AI that together lead to an exponential increase in opportunities for businesses across sectors. Firstly, generative AI is inherently scalable. It can process vast amounts of data and generate insights or create outputs much more efficiently than humans, potentially leading to massive productivity gains and cost savings. For instance, AI can streamline supply chains by predicting demand trends, or it can enhance customer service by powering chatbots that handle routine queries round-the-clock. Secondly, AI can learn and improve autonomously. Given enough data and computational power, it can identify patterns, make predictions, and even create new content with minimal human intervention. This ability to "learn" enables AI to continuously adapt and improve, thereby constantly creating new value. Thirdly, the versatility of AI applications is staggering. From healthcare to finance to entertainment, AI can add value in diverse ways in virtually every sector. It can generate personalized recommendations for customers, assist doctors in diagnosing diseases, automate accounting tasks, create new music or art, and much more. Moreover, the innovative applications of AI can lead to the creation of entirely new products, services, and business models, opening up novel revenue streams. For instance, organizations are already leveraging AI to offer personalized digital content, predictive maintenance services, and AI-powered software solutions. Another important aspect is the ability of AI to "amplify" human capabilities. By automating routine tasks and generating insights from data, AI can free up humans to focus on tasks that require creativity, critical thinking, and emotional intelligence.

The value creation potential of AI holds promise for addressing grand challenges such as sustainability. By leveraging AI's analytical power, we can drive the transition towards a more sustainable and resilient future. However, it is essential to recognize that AI is not a panacea, and its implementation must be guided by ethical considerations, transparency, and inclusive decision-making. Through collaborative efforts, leveraging the potential of AI responsibly can unlock innovative solutions and pave the way for a sustainable and thriving world.

As we face pressing grand challenges – like climate change, resource depletion, and environmental degradation, harnessing the power of AI can facilitate innovative solutions, enable smarter decision-making, and ultimately propel us towards a sustainable future. The sheer volume and complexity of data related to climate, ecosystems, energy consumption, and resource management necessitate advanced analytical tools to derive meaningful information. AI can help integrate data from multiple sources, model complex systems, and provide predictive analytics, empowering researchers, policymakers, and businesses with the knowledge required for informed decision-making. In addition, AI has the potential to revolutionize energy consumption and resource management. Intelligent algorithms can optimize energy usage, minimizing waste, and improving efficiency in industries, transportation, and residential sectors. AI-powered systems can monitor and control energy-intensive processes in real-time, adjusting parameters to achieve optimal performance. Moreover, AI-driven optimization algorithms can enable resource allocation and utilization, reducing waste, and maximizing productivity. AI can also play a vital role in ensuring the smooth integration and optimal utilization of renewable energy systems. By analyzing weather patterns, energy demand, and supply dynamics, AI algorithms can predict renewable energy generation and optimize its integration into existing power grids. Such insights can enhance grid stability, enable demand-response mechanisms, and facilitate efficient energy storage, accelerating the adoption of renewable energy on a larger scale.

AI's ability to process vast amounts of data, identify patterns, and generate insights offers invaluable advantages in tackling challenges for organizations. This can lead to improved decision-making, innovation, and customer relationships, which in turn create substantial value. Finally, as AI technologies continue to advance, they will unlock even more possibilities for value creation.

Innovations in AI research and increasing computational power will lead to AI systems that are more capable, efficient, and versatile. In particular, advances in areas like natural language understanding and reinforcement learning could revolutionize how AI is used in business. As such, generative AI offers a pathway to value creation for organizations. It can create value in ways we can currently envision, but perhaps more importantly, it also holds the potential to create value in ways we cannot even imagine yet.

Appendix 1
AI readiness questionnaire

AI Readiness Score		None	Low	Moderate	High	Excellent
Technologies						
Present	Our present AI technology portfolio adds value to our organization					
Future	We have a strategy for using our AI technology portfolio to add value to our organization					
Activities						
Present	Our present key activities are supported by AI in ways that add value to our organization					
Future	We have a strategy for using AI to support key activities in ways that add value to our organization					
Boundaries						
Present	Our present organizational boundaries are stretched by AI use in ways that add value to our organization					
Future	We have a strategy for using AI to change our organizational boundaries in ways that add value to our organization					
Goals						
Present	Our present AI use supports our goals in ways that add value to our organization					
Future	We have a strategy for using AI to support our goals in ways that add value to our organization					

Appendix 2

Data strategy questionnaire

	Evaluation of data work domain				
Question	**None**	**Low**	**Medium**	**High**	**Excellent**
We have internal competence in place for our data work					
We have internal technologies in place for our data work					
We have ways to leverage value from our internal competence and technologies for our data work					
We have access to additional external competence available for our data work					
We have access to additional external technologies available for our data work					
We have ways to leverage value from additional competence and technologies in our data work					
	Evaluation of data source				
Question	**None**	**Low**	**Medium**	**High**	**Excellent**
We have existing data sources available for our data work					
We have competence to leverage our existing data sources in our data work					
We have technologies to leverage our existing data sources in our data work					
We have new data sources available for our data work					
We have competence to leverage our new data sources in our data work					
We have technologies to leverage our new data sources in our data work					

References

Aaltonen, A., Alaimo, C., & Kallinikos, J. (2021). The making of data commodities: Data analytics as an embedded process. *Journal of Management Information Systems, 38*(2), 401–429.

Agrawal, A., Gans, J., & Goldfarb, A. (2018). Algorithms and human experts: Complementarity in medical imaging. *Management Science, 64*(9), 4035–4051.

Alaimo, C., & Kallinikos, J. (2022). Organizations decentered: Data objects, technology and knowledge. *Organization Science, 33*(1), 19–37.

Allen, R., & Choudhury, P. (2022). Algorithm-augmented work and domain experience: The countervailing forces of ability and aversion. *Organization Science, 33*(1), 149–169.

Amoore, L. (2020). *Cloud ethics: Algorithms and the attributes of ourselves and others*. Duke University Press.

Anderson, C. (2008). The end of theory: The data deluge makes the scientific method obsolete. *Wired Magazine, 16*(7), 16. https://www.wired.com/2008/06/pb-theory/

Baskerville, R., Myers, M. D., & Yoo, Y. (2020). Digital first: The ontological reversal and new challenges for IS research. *MIS Quarterly, 44*(2), 509–523.

Berente, N., Gu, B., Recker, J., & Santhanam, R. (2021). Special issue editor's comments: Managing artificial intelligence. *Management Information Systems Quarterly, 45*(3), 1433–1450.

Bostrom, N. (2014). *Superintelligence: Paths, dangers, strategies*. Oxford Univ. Press.

Brynjolfsson, E., & McAfee, A. (2014). *The second machine age: Work, progress, and prosperity in a time of brilliant technologies*. WW Norton & Company.

Carroll, N., Holmström, J., Stahl, B. C., & Fabian, N. E. (2024). Navigating the utopia and dystopia perspectives of artificial intelligence. *Communications of the Association for Information Systems, 55*(1), 32.

Choudhury, P., Starr, E., & Agarwal, R. (2020). Machine learning and human capital complementarities: Experimental evidence on bias mitigation. *Strategic Management Journal, 41*(8), 1381–1411.

Christensen, C. M. (2013). *The innovator's dilemma: when new technologies cause great firms to fail*. Harvard Business Review Press.

Crawford, K. (2021). *The atlas of AI: Power, politics, and the planetary costs of artificial intelligence*. Yale University Press.

Dreyfus, H. L. (1972). *What computers can't do*. Harper & Row.

Ehn, P. (1988). Work-oriented design of computer artifacts, Stockholm: Arbetslivscentrum.

Farjoun, M., & Mahmood, N. (2023). On habit and organizing: A transactional perspective relating firms, consumers, and social institutions. *Organization Science*, *35*(3), 1157.

Feuerriegel, S., Shrestha, Y. R., von Krogh, G., & Zhang, C. (2022). Bringing artificial intelligence to business management. *Nature Machine Intelligence*, *4*(7), 611–613.

Frey, C. B., & Osborne, M. A. (2017). The future of employment: How susceptible are jobs to computerisation? *Technological Forecasting and Social Change*, *114*, 254–280.

Gupta, A., & Tu, Q. (2020). AI and the social sciences: Opportunities and challenges. *Journal of Artificial Intelligence Research*, *67*, 789–813.

Holmström, J. (2022). From AI to digital transformation: The AI readiness framework. *Business Horizons*, *65*(3), 329–339.

Holmström, J., & Carroll, N. (2025). How organizations can innovate with generative AI. *Business Horizons*, *68*, 559–573.

Holmström, J., & Magnusson, J. (2025). *Navigating the organizational AI journey: The AI transformation framework*. Business Horizons.

Ibrahim, R., Kim, S. H., & Tong, J. (2021). Eliciting human judgment for prediction algorithms. *Management Science*, *67*(4), 2314–2325.

Johnson, M., & Vera, A. (2019). No AI is an island: The case for teaming intelligence. *AI Magazine*, *40*(1), 16–28.

Kahneman, D. (2011). *Thinking, fast and slow*. Macmillan.

Lebovitz, S., Levina, N., & Lifshitz-Assaf, H. (2021). Is AI ground truth really true? The dangers of training and evaluating AI tools based on experts' know-what. *Management Information Systems Quarterly*, *45*(3), 1501–1526.

LeCun, Y., Bengio, Y., & Hinton, G. (2015). Deep learning. *Nature*, *521*(7553), 436–444.

Lindgren, S., & Holmström, J. (2020). A social science perspective on artificial intelligence: Building blocks for a research agenda. *Journal of Digital Social Research*, *2*(3), 1–15.

Miller, P., Domingos, P., & Kim, B. (2017). AI as a social science. *Communications of the ACM*, *60*(9), 96–104.

Monteiro, E. (2022). *Digital oil: Machineries of knowing*. MIT Press.

O'Neil, C. (2017). *Weapons of math destruction: How big data increases inequality and threatens democracy*. Crown.

Parmiggiani, E., Østerlie, T., & Almklov, P. G. (2022). In the backrooms of data science. *Journal of the Association for Information Systems*, *23*(1), 139–164.

Paschen, U., Pitt, C., & Kietzmann, J. (2020). Artificial intelligence: Building blocks and an innovation typology. *Business Horizons*, *63*(2), 147–155.

Ransbotham, S., Kiron, D., Gerbert, P., & Reeves, M. (2017). Reshaping business with artificial intelligence: Closing the gap between ambition and action. *MIT Sloan Management Review*, *59*(1), 1–17.

Russell, S., & Norvig, P. (2002). *Artificial intelligence: A modern approach* (2nd ed.). Prentice Hall.

Sundberg, L., & Holmström, J. (2022a). Are AI opportunities discovered or created? Investigating data resourcing using a no-code AI platform in an educational context. In *Americas Conference on Information Systems* (AMCIS 2022), Article 1209. Association for Information Systems.https://aisel.aisnet.org/amcis2022/sig_ed/sig_ed/11/

Sundberg, L., & Holmström, J. (2022b). Towards 'lightweight' artificial intelligence: A typology of AI service platforms. In *Americas Conference on Information Systems* (AMCIS 2022). Association for Information Systems.

Sundberg, L., & Holmström, J. (2023). Democratizing artificial intelligence: How no-code AI can leverage machine learning operations. *Business Horizons*, *66*(6), 777–788.

Villegas-Galaviz, C., & Martin, K. (2023). Moral distance, AI, and the ethics of care. *AI & Society*, *39*(4), 1695–1706.

Index

Note: Page numbers in **bold** reference tables. Page numbers in *italics* reference figures.abilities of AI 14–15